The TWENTY SECRETS
of SUCCESS

By FENWICKE L. HOLMES

Publisher
Spirit Rising, Inc.
One Science of Mind Way
Asheville, NC   28806
2018

Originally Published By
Robert M. Mcbride & Company
7 West Sixteenth Street New York
1927

For additional books, audio and
video recordings visit CSLAsheville.org

Table of Contents

INTRODUCTION

ARE some born to the hovel and others to the hotel, some to the ditch and others to the dutchy? Has the divine economy arranged that of two, born side by side, one is designed to be "waiter" and the other to be waited upon? No greater falsehood was ever perpetrated upon the human race than the promulgation of such a doctrine.

On the other hand, a second lie has been conceived to combat the first, to wit, that everyone has an equal right with every other, not to the reward of his own brain and toil, but to the brain and toil of others.

The fact is that what a man is to possess has not been arbitrarily settled upon by a designing Creator. It has been put under a fixed and invariable principle which is no respecter of persons and metes out to each according to his use of the law of getting and keeping. For while there is plenty of all for each, he obtains it only in proportion to his knowledge and use of the law of financial freedom, which rewards those who obey the rules and deprives those who break them.

We are all "to the manor born," and the difference in degree of possession is not to be measured by privilege but by the development of capacity which enables each

CSLAsheville.org

to make a more or less intelligent demand upon an equally impersonal law.

It is said by some that it is hard to make money, and that those who do make it usually have no deference to the decalog. As a matter of fact, the making of money is no more difficult than the harvesting of any other crop whose seed we have planted. The analogy is perfect, for we literally "reap as we have sown," and if we know how to sow the seeds of success, we shall reap it. To know what this seed is, to sow it, and consequently to reap the harvest, is to put oneself in the possession of wealth. Nor will he resent its possession by another when he has made plenty of his own. The universe is full of the raw materials of wealth and plenty, so that there is enough for all. It only remains to learn the secret of its acquisition, to lift the world out of poverty and want.

The great seers of the past have understood this law and have declared that "whatsoever a man soweth that shall he also reap," but it has not generally been considered that the statement refers to anything else than religion. It has remained for the present day to investigate the psychological, metaphysical, and financial law that underlies this statement, and present it as a science to the human race. As H. G. Wells has remarked, in effect, "The next century will be a century of applied psychology." We have the materials and the machinery of universal financial freedom. We must cultivate the knowledge which will utilize them for the good of each.

This knowledge is psychological and metaphysical, and it is our purpose in the present volume of this series to show how those who aspire to financial freedom may develop and employ the necessary mental qualities to produce complete economic independence and soul-satisfying environment for themselves and those who are dear to them.

This volume is the book of personal development and the law of psychology applied to the attainment of financial freedom.

FENWICKE L. HOLMES.

San Francisco, California, September 7, 1926

Chapter 1 FINANCIAL FREEDOM AND MONEY

MONEY is a word of magic. Speak it with authority and the world will bring its rarest treasures to your door,—its wood cut in the depth of swamps or primeval forests and cunningly wrought and finished; its finely-carded wool woven on ancient looms in far-away places; its silks spun by insects and patterned by man; its skins from the remotest wilderness; its ores grubbed from the heart of the earth and fashioned into half-human bodies to wash and sew, to drive your wheels and take you hither and yon; its canvases touched to life by the soul of the artist; its songs and melodies; its feasts and festivals. These are the treasures which the magic of money will draw to your door.

Is it any wonder that all the world is interested in money, eager to learn the secret of the acquisition of wealth? And why should we assume that it is wrong for the spiritually minded to inquire into it? Is all money "tainted"? Are they alone saintly who live without food, shelter, and beauty? Character is not a problem of money but a question of method. There are those who have character and no money, others who have money and no character; there are those who have both, and there are those who have neither. I propose to show that it is possible to obtain one without losing the other, how it is done by mental law; and how each individual may possess all he desires without robbing any other.

Money is power. Money is freedom. Money is a universal solvent. Money is a god that settles disputes, heals wounds and fosters brotherhood; it is a devil that makes war and in its frenzy feeds on its own vitals. Money is a crucifix or a cannon, a palace or a prison, a friend or a foe. But it is always a force.

Money is houses, lands, railways, ships, services, honors, ease, travel. Money is nothing. Now we get down to the meat of it. Money is nothing! A barrel of marks may not be worth a bottle of beer, a liter of lira, not worth the trouble of figuring the exchange. But the same may be said of a paper dollar, or a thousand dollar bill! If you doubt this, note what happens to the man who removes the "one" from a dollar bill and reprints it with two ciphers. Nothing is changed but the ink; but when the government superscription is gone, it is "all gone." The value of money in itself is the value of the paper on which it is printed. Money is nothing.

Money is mutual agreement, cooperation, coordination, confidence, faith. Money is faith. It is the belief men have in each other. The word creed and the word credit both come from the same Latin root, "credo," I believe. When I take money from you in exchange for my labor it is because of my belief. I believe that when I take this money to the grocer he will give me flour; to the baker, he will give me bread; to the tailor, he will give me clothes. I believe that each of them will believe in my money.

Money is a symbol. It symbolizes the labor you have performed, the crops you raised, the goods you manufactured; the book you wrote, the picture you painted, the song you sang, the sermon you preached. It is a sign, the sign of boiled-down labor of brains or brawn. It is a symbol of the exchange you are about to make, your brawn for another's brains, your brains for another's brawn.

Money is service. The world pays for whatever it values—a trinket, a car, a painting, a teacher, a preacher, a dream, a thought. The world always wants something; whatever it wants it must pay for, and whatever it pays for it must want or it would not pay for it. Therefore whoever satisfies a want becomes a servant, and his services must receive their hire.

Summing it all up, then, money is the symbol of service.

There are many kinds of services, but all of them can be turned first into the symbol or medium of exchange which we call money and then back into services and things. In this form it becomes a great force. It is power and this power is neutral. That is, the money can become anything we want it to become. That is why the world wants money so that it can have not what anyone happens to give it, but what it wants to get.

Money is freedom to do what we want to do, to go where we want to go, and to be what we want to be. There is nothing bad in money, for who can see wrong in a symbol of service which is a great, impersonal force, inspiring faith and convertible into other forms which the possessor can creatively mold into whatsoever he wills?

 The wrong associated with money lies not in the money but the association—how it was gained and how it is spent.

Was it acquired in honorable service, is it spent for honorable ends? Is the labor worth the hire, or did he who gained the hire lose his own soul in the acquisition? And what is it to "lose one's own soul"?

 It is evident from the foregoing that money is simply a convenient method of Transformation, the medium in which we dissolve one form and bring forth another.

Form is transferred into energy or force and from energy or force refashioned into form. Just as we cast all our old trinkets into the crucible and remold them into a dish or a statue so we cast all our possessions into the matrix called money and bring forth other desired forms. Of course there are other and more primitive methods of exchange. I may saw wood for my dinner or exchange a sonnet for a saw. Or I may repudiate money as "the root of all evil" and say to my employer, "I will trust you tomorrow to give me bread for the work I did yesterday." To so repudiate money is to deny myself the conveniences of civilization. Only the ignorant or the fanatical, therefore, will dispense with the services of money; and this book is not written for either.

It is not money, but "the love of money," that is the "root of all evil." The quest of a competence in the medium of money is, therefore, legitimate, and the only moral or ethical question that may be raised is, "How did you get it?"

Chapter 2 MONEY, SOULS, AND PSYCHOLOGY

MONEY is not wealth. It is one of the symbols of wealth. What, then, is wealth? Wealth is the ownership of something the world wants and for which it will exchange its labor, money, or property. In general, it means possessing something that is useful. Or it may mean having something which is not useful now but which can be made useful. That is called potential wealth. Mines, oil fields, vacant land, water power, concessions, inventions, "undeveloped resources," may become wealth, and have their value because you, yourself, and others have faith in them. The greatest wealth of America today lies in her undeveloped resources. Potentially there is enough to sustain ten times the present population.

There was a time when all the wealth of the world was only potential. It lay like a fallow field waiting for the seed. Economic wealth is the product of man's mind and muscle united with the forces of nature. Wealth, therefore, is something that can be created.

There are many ways to get rich but it is important to remember that wealth can be "created," that it must be something useful, and that the employment of the mind is essential to it.

The difference between savage races and civilized, between those who have potential wealth and those who have created wealth, lies in the mental equation. The natural resources are awaiting the mind of the thinker. The field must be seeded with psychology. Brains are in demand. Thoughts are at a premium. The reaction requires a catalyzer. That catalyzer is mind. That mind may be yours.

In considering how you may use your mind to acquire wealth, it is very essential that you learn to use it in the right way so that you may avoid failure and extract the greatest measure of results from the least effort. There is a right way and a wrong way to use the mind. There is a law of mind and we succeed or fail as we obey the requirements of this law. Those who are ignorant of this law are handicapped by their ignorance. Those who are acquainted with it possess an asset. It is interesting to note that a national training organization, doing all its teaching by mail, has increased the average earnings of its graduates by almost one hundred percent. That shows what the mental element may become in the attainment of success, for the student's wealth is increased not by added material and economic capital but by drawing upon his undeveloped mental resources.

It is not our purpose here to teach the technique of business or vocation. That belongs to the schools or to experience. Our purpose is to show how you may take yourself in hand, employ your present technical knowledge or material possessions, and by the addition of the new knowledge of mental law, increase your wealth. And this may be done without the sacrifice of your higher ideals but rather in perfect harmony with them. In fact, it will be found that those who follow these principles will gradually develop deeper spiritual qualities because they are seeking to put all their forces into expression; and the mobilization of all your resources must of necessity include your spiritual forces. And strange as it may seem, a large part of the failures in modern life, including business, vocation, health, and happiness, is due to ignorance of the deeper qualities and laws of our nature. Recent discoveries in the field of psychology, especially in psychoanalysis, have revealed the fact that a large percent of those who fail to "make good" owe their failure to ignorance or neglect of the fact that they have a soul.

One can imagine the howl of derision that would have greeted this statement ten years ago. The religious would have stigmatized it "prostitution," and the scientific would have stigmatized it as religious. As a matter of fact, it is now well known among psychological experts, including psychiatrists, vocational advisers, and psychoanalysts, that neurotics and failures owe their condition largely and often entirely to the fact that they are "misfits." They are "not adapted," not vocationally adjusted. They are doing something for which they are not "naturally" fitted. The "self" or "psyche" is not satisfied; the mind is distressed by the constant effort to do something distasteful to it—and so the psyche "gets sick," the body gets sick, and the business gets sick

We shall consider this in the next chapter.

Chapter 3 WEALTH AND SELF-EXPRESSION

AN Italian laborer in Los Angeles spent twenty years digging sewers. During that time he carried suspended about his neck a bag containing "a good luck stone," a little red thing he had picked up. One day a glint of color caught the eye of an onlooker. The bag was opened and "the little red thing" proved to be a pigeon ruby. It was worth $20,000. For twenty years this man had dug in dirt, lived in squalor, and fed on the fare of poverty in ignorance of his hidden fortune.

The story stirs us like an adventure. The pathos! The ignorance! The labor! The lost years! The unrecognized resources! But a greater story should stir us—the story of this man is the story of humanity. We all possess potential wealth, uncapitalized and unrecognized. But deep within us there is "something that knows," something that urges us on to become more, have more, live more. That something is the soul,—the ego, the psyche,—seeking self-expression and freedom. Fed on the fare of poverty, it starves! Hidden from the eye of sense, it yet contrives to send forth a gleam, demanding recognition.

One of the most startling discoveries in the realm of nature is the uniqueness of all things. There is no sameness in nature. There is likeness or similarity, there is uniformity of law, but there is no absolute reduplication. It has been said that after God makes a great man like Lincoln, He breaks the mold. After God makes anything, He breaks the mold.

There are no two things exactly alike in all the world, and there are no two souls alike. Your resources are individual, your personality is singular. You are come into the world to add your bit to the great mosaic of humanity, to weave your thread on the loom of the race. The thread may be gold or gray, foreground or background, but it is yours, and the pattern will not be complete without it.

How do we know that the soul has a purpose? The purpose of the soul is the root of revelation recently supported by the science of psychology. Whatever man has been able to discover intuitively regarding the meaning of life has always indicated the soul as being on a quest. It is here on a mission and woe to that soul that bears not its message! Recent studies in psychology have corroborated this intuition. That the psyche has designs for self-accomplishment is shown in the way it acts when thwarted—it proceeds to get sick and by the laws of the externalization of thought makes the body sick with it.

We will suppose that you have an instinctive interest in writing. From your earliest years, you have dreamed of some day becoming a writer. You have taken pleasure in forming your thoughts and building beautiful words around them. You have loved language and you have been filled with romance. "Tomorrow" you were going to write a book. But tomorrow came empty-handed and demanded bread instead of words. So you worked for bread.

Tomorrow you would write but this time she demanded shelter or clothes, or a bottle for the baby. So the years come and go but tomorrow never comes bringing you a day and a pencil and paper. Your soul, which is here to write books, begins to droop; its wistful eye, which has greeted so many disappointing tomorrows, is dulled; hope can no longer sustain the illusions of tomorrow. The psyche "gets sick."

Chapter 4 SUGGESTION

THE vast majority of the human race is ruled not by reason and logic but by emotion and imagination. The orator who is ignorant of this principle will find his most brilliant arguments and learning no match for the "spellbinder" or demagogue who does not know one-tenth as much about the subject but does know how to sway the mind of the mob.[1] Of course, knowledge of the subject is indispensable to advancement and, if coupled with the art of making an emotional appeal, will create an irresistible leader. William Jennings Bryan and Robert La Follette were outstanding examples of this during the last quarter of the nineteenth century and the first quarter of the twentieth.

We do not "think" half as much as we "feel." Thinking is a comparatively recent accomplishment in human evolution, while feeling began with protoplasmic life. Most of the things we do are not done as the result of conscious thought and well-ordered planning but merely from habit. We are largely controlled by our tendency to do things as we used to do them, as our neighbors do them, and as our fathers and mothers

---

[1] See "The Mob" by Le Mott

before us did them. As a usual thing we rather dislike new ways, new things, new ideas, because they are unfamiliar to us. They make us uncomfortable. All important changes are brought about with great discomfort, much mental resistance. The progress of the race is realized largely through the zeal and self-sacrifice of one or more individuals who force the new ideas on the multitudes, usually at the sacrifice of their own comfort and often of their own lives. "Never man so spoke," said the soldiers in reporting their failure to take Jesus, but his contemporaries crucified him. It was not the masterful logic of the Master which finally won him a place in spiritual leadership of the race, but the remarkable appeal to the imagination and the emotions made by his tragic death and the fanatical devotion of his disciples, all but one of whom sacrificed his life for the message.

This tendency to be swayed by the imagination is the primary factor of what we call "suggestion." It can be observed in many forms. A child has the instinctive tendency to imitate what its parents and others around it do and say. It is controlled not by reason but by the "suggestions" of its environment. Mother's way of keeping house becomes the daughter's way, and even the instruction of the teacher in the domestic science department of the schools, though reinforced by emulation and example of fellow-students is hardly strong enough to change the child's idea of what is natural or right, and it goes on "in the same old way." The strong suggestion of companionship is shown in the way some boys will immediately become whatever their playmates are "without rhyme or reason." The theater exercises a strong suggestive power and we speak of a play as "suggestive" if it contains lines or scenes which tend to arouse improper thoughts or feelings. It is for this reason that many people feel that the stage and the screen should be carefully censored.

Suggestion plays an important part in the art of advertising and salesmanship. The effort of the salesman is to impart an idea to the mind of the buyer in such a way as to arouse his interest and encourage his decision to buy. When, for example, a saleswoman puts a cloak on a possible customer, and says, "How well that shade or style becomes you!" she is using the art of suggestion, because she is arousing the desire and decision to buy.

Suggestion, then, may be defined as the art of conveying an idea from one mind to another in such a way as to arouse response and action of some kind or at least the acceptance of a point of view which was not previously held, as when the preacher succeeds in converting or proselyting. To be a true suggestion, it must reach the subconscious mind of the subject in such a way as to be actually embedded there. Motor action or permanent change is the result. This is particularly true in the matter of healing by suggestion, which is not, as many suppose, a modern art, but is better understood than it was a thousand or more years ago. In the case of healing by suggestion, ideas are transferred to the mind of the patient which supplant other ideas he holds about himself. The modem method is to have the patient take an easy position, assume a half sleepy attitude while the physician speaks in a low and rather monotonous tone, declaring that the old idea of pain, disease, and inharmony is now being replaced with health and wholeness. He usually describes the new condition which is to manifest in the patient. This is called suggestion or psychotherapeutics. Those who call themselves spiritual healers often repudiate the term "suggestion" and call that "mental science" as opposed to their system of healing. It is instructive, however, in this connection to note that Mrs. Eddy says, "Christian Science explains all cause and effect as mental, not physical."[2] Her theory merely reverses the suggestion, for she conceives that the patient is already suggested or hypnotized into the belief he is sick and her method is to remove this suggestion or hypnotic idea. This is

---

[2] My own point of view on this matter will be found in my book, "The Law of Mind in Action."

accomplished by conveying the suggestion that the sickness is only a belief and that when this is accepted or realized, the patient will find himself well.

Suggestion is a scientific fact and it is useless to take an antagonistic attitude toward it as though there were something wrong in its use. It is not the control of a stronger mind over a weaker one, nor a method of getting the best of another by mental means. Like all laws it will work in either direction and can be used to further either good or bad ends. It is a method of awakening the deepest forces of the mind to action along the chosen line. When applied to oneself, it is called autosuggestion. It may be one which uproots and removes a former destructive suggestion, leaving the mind to act in a normal or healthy state, thus producing a healthy body (as in healing by the metaphysical method followed by Mental Science, Christian Science, Divine Science, etc.), or it may initiate an entirely new train of ideas and actions. It may be used to heal the body,—bring about social, political, or religious changes,—promote or obstruct progress,—further business success either in advertising, salesmanship, or profession. Ignorance of it is a handicap; knowledge, a handmaiden.

We are all trying to bring about changes that will better our condition and we should avail ourselves of the magic power of suggestion and learn how to use it in the wisest and most constructive way possible. We should learn how to eliminate from our mind ail ideas that tend to failure, and plant in their place the sturdy seed of success.

A TREATMENT BY SUGGESTION

The following suggestion or treatment will be of value: I know that there is nothing to obstruct my progress. There is no force pitted against me and there is no bad luck lying in wait for me. Nothing happens by chance and I will not accept the idea that I am governed by any circumstance or condition. I am the maker and therefore the master of conditions, and I am the ruler of my own fate. From this time on I am going to look only for the constructive and helpful ideas, situation, and people. I am going to believe in myself. I am going to be happy in the realization that "all power is given unto me" to be what I want to be, to go where I want to go, and to do what I want to do. I am thankful for the opportunities that lie before me and for the intelligence which will henceforth guide me in taking advantage of them.

"Mind is the master power that molds and makes, and man is mind, and evermore he takes the tools of thought and shaping what he wills brings forth a thousand joys, a thousand ills. He thinks in secret and it

comes to pass; Environment is but his looking-glass."

Chapter 5 THE NECESSITY OF CHOOSING WHAT WE WANT

A "SUGGESTION" may be likened to a seed which we plant in the ground. The earth is a vast potential power that contains within itself nourishment and moisture, ready to become a tree, a rose, a bramble, or a thistle. But it lies fallow, waiting for the seed. It is able to bring forth what you call good or to bring forth bad. It can enrich or impoverish you, not by any choices of its own but by the very fidelity with which it grows what you choose to plant. It has no choices of its own. It never says within itself, "He has planted calla lilies but I will bring forth skunk cabbages"; or, "He has ignorantly sowed thistles but I will grow figs." Somewhere Troward has said, "Seed of one kind will never bring forth fruit of another." Yet many are praying that it may and wondering why the Almighty "allows so much suffering and poverty in the world."

As a matter of fact, the suffering and poverty of the world are not the choice of the Almighty but the result of our own choices. "There are two sides to everything." The Sphinx of existence has two faces, and the power of choice is given each of us to "follow his nose." We may go up or down, in or out, right or wrong; we may be happy or unhappy, well or sick, provident or prodigal; we may be "sweet as an angel" or "act like the devil." It follows that success or failure depends upon the choices we make, the seed we plant, or the suggestions which we give to others or to ourselves. Yet how many there are who, knowing this, will continue to say, "I never have a chance." "I would like to but——" "I may succeed up to a certain point but after that——" "A poor man has no chance these days." "I haven't enough capital to make a success." "I cannot decide what I should do." "Let's leave it to chance." "They all rob you." "The capitalistic system grinds us down." "Times are bad and getting worse." "Money is tight." "Competition is destroying my business." "Nobody appreciates me and everybody is out for 'number one' "—and so on and on.

Study yourself to see what your negative suggestions are. Do you not see that you are giving yourself suggestions that are destroying your business or vocation, and that the seeds of your failure are being sown far and wide? Do you not see that you are really "treating yourself" for disaster and that "you will reap what you sow"? Will you not make up your mind to eliminate these negative thoughts and in their place sow the seed of faith in yourself and others and belief that you can and will?

Today is the "great day of the Lord" if you will it so. Make up your mind as to what you wish to be and do. Do not "leave it to chance," for to leave it to chance merely means that you are going to wait until some suggestion enters the mind without your conscious thought. This may be a good suggestion or a bad one. It may be creative or destructive. It may be for your benefit or another's. Why let some other mind decide? Why let someone "use you" because you do not have sense enough to use yourself?

Decide what is to be the great aim of your life and let no thought enter your mind but success. You must know what you want for it is not given anyone else to know that for you. If you do not know it consciously, still it lies as potential knowledge within you and there is a way to find it out. Make up your mind to the big issue!

SUGGESTION TO BE REALIZED

I have the power of choice and the ability to choose. There is a way for me to do what I want to do, and I am going to find it. I will henceforth decide on what I want and go ahead in confidence to do it. From this day I will stop all negative suggestions. I will not see, hear, nor speak anything that will suggest failure. I am success.

Chapter 6 THE SUBCONSCIOUS MIND

WE have seen that there is a tendency in all of us to react in a definite way to thoughts or ideas which we call suggestion. After we become thoroughly acquainted with a man, we feel that we can "depend on him," as we say, which merely means that we know pretty well how he will act under given circumstances, "how he will feel about it'," and what he will do. In other words, wc know in general the sum-total of his habits of thought. The same is true of society. We become acquainted with any race, nation, or group, and we learn that the vast majority holds similar ideas, accepts the same customs and standards, and has similar religious concepts. If it were not so, and if every individual on earth had different customs and views from every other, social intercourse would be impossible, and we would be totally unable to "understand" each other. Because we know in general the sum-total of the habits of society we can usually tell in advance how it will react to any given idea.

We may speak of this sum-total of mental habits both of the individual and of society as the subconscious mind. It is the mental activity which takes place without conscious thought; it is intelligence acting "unthinkingly." But it is intelligence in some form for it reacts to ideas or suggestions, and in an orderly way which we can understand.

Knowledge of the existence of this corporate or social subconscious is important for it points the way to the proper use of suggestion to sway not merely one mind but many. This is well illustrated in the art of advertising. The best advertisement is, of course, the one which will attract the largest number of purchasers for the least money. It has been found by experience that the following make the most striking appeal: Necessities of life, as things to eat and wear; things that promote the sense of power and importance of the individual, such as a better house, neighborhood, or car than one's neighbors or associates; love of out-of-doors, which is instinctive.

In other words, the suggestion to be made by the advertiser or salesman is merely a reinforcement of the suggestion which the possible buyer has already been making to himself.

On the other hand, if it is something new that is to be promoted, it becomes necessary to make a "campaign of suggestion." The public must be informed that the article exists, is for sale, and has virtues which make its possession desirable. It must be talked about, read about, seen, and if by any means possible, discussed. It is especially desirable to have it argued over, and in the case of a new religious idea, for example, it fosters growth to have it quarreled about. Partisanship means patronage. New ideas must become familiar before accepted or paid for. James A. Garfield used to say that an unfamiliar idea had to be presented three times in the same speech. The third time it became acceptable because familiar. It has been proven by actual tests that an advertisement of a quarter page inserted four times in the newspaper will bring five times the result secured by a full page of the same advertisement if inserted but once. The suggestion becomes more powerful each time it is made until the reader remembers it and feels an impulse to buy. Repetition of suggestion is, therefore, seen as an imperative.

Our minds are being impinged upon constantly by suggestions and to a very great extent we rule or are ruled by them. It is well from time to time to run over the chief factors in our lives to see whether or not we belong to the vast group who "act without thinking." Are we just accepting whatever suggestion comes our way or are we resolutely formulating our own suggestions, establishing our own standards, and marking out our own pathway? Ninety-five percent of Americans, to say nothing of foreign peoples, are led by the other five percent. The "other five" owns most of the wealth. Who is deciding your social, religious, political, and economic ideas and ideals for you?

Possibly it is time to wake up and think! The thinkers are those who formulate the suggestions for the unthinking.

Read what Mr. Henry Ford says in his book, "My Life and Work," under the title, "Machines and Men":

"Scarcely more than five percent of those who work for wages, while they have the desire to receive more money, have also the willingness to accept additional responsibility and the additional work which goes with the high places."

Responsibility means independence, and independence means the selection and formulation of your own suggestions.

A number of years ago the author of this book was conducting lectures and classes as one of the directors of the Southern California Metaphysical Institute. In line with what we have just been saying, he conducted the following experiment. A series of lecture lessons on scientific salesmanship was prepared; a theater was rented; admission was made without charge, and an expert salesman was sent out with literature to the department stores and other places where labor was employed to invite those interested to attend. So few accepted the invitation that the number was negligible and had it not been for our large membership and personal following, the experiment would have been very costly. It was to me a very graphic demonstration of the reason why five percent is rich and the other ninety-five per cent is poor.

This book is written for those who are determined to join the leaders of the race. Be willing to think. Few do.

> *"How few there be of the thinking few*
> *Who really think, who think they do."*

How very few, then, are those who think!

Re-educate your subconscious by suggestion. Declare many times daily, "I will henceforth refuse to think that I cannot succeed. I will no longer be hypnotized by the following ideas. (Name the ones you are going to get rid of.) I can and will succeed along this line." (Name the things you desire to accomplish and firmly hold them in mind as certain of accomplishment.)

Chapter 7 SUGGESTION AND THE SUBCONSCIOUS MIND

FOR those of us who have come to the reluctant but reasonable conclusion that we are stupid, there is no more astonishing revelation than that of modern psychology regarding the unconscious activity of intelligence which we call the subconscious. We bewail our forgetfulness, but the memory of the subconscious is perfect, it never forgets. A permanent impression is made upon it by every experience, every word, every transitory thought; and though we may fail in every conscious effort to recall it, still the deeper strata of mind retain the cryptic intelligence and will reveal it either by a sudden "recollection," or in abnormal mental states such as in fever, trance, or automatic writing.[3]

We may require someone to "show us the way to go home," but the subconscious intelligence contains a subtle power to direct the flight of the bird, the course of the spawning salmon through the uncharted seas; and it will do the same thing for man, bringing him

---

[3] See my "Textbook of Psychology and Metaphysics," pp. 19-27; Maeterlinck's, "The Great Secret"; Prince, "The Unconscious," p. 53

into safety when he relies upon it, whether it be in actual physical directions or in the selection of the course of action he should pursue.[4] Wise, indeed, is that man or woman who learns how to plumb the depths of his own mind and employ this marvelous power which will help him in all the problems of life

A mere enumeration of some of the qualities of the subconscious mind should awaken our interest and enthusiasm for further study and employment of its forces. It has the power to transmit or record thought without physical medium, as in "mental telepathy," even to great distances.[5]

---

[4] See my "Textbook," p. 2. Also my "Law of Mind in Action," Chap. XXIX
Also Chap. VI, Vol, II, of this series, "How to Choose a Career."

[5] See Chap. III, Vol. II, of this Series, "Visualization and Concentration."

It possesses the power of clairvoyance, or seeing without the physical eye; clairaudience, perceiving sound beyond the reach of the ear.[6]

Subconsciousness explains the secret of psychometry, reading the history of an object by touching it or diagnosing disease by occult mental perception.[7]

The presence of this consciousness is revealed in such phenomena as automatic writing; in hypnosis; somnambulism, or sleep-walking; and in dreams.[8]

The term subconsciousness covers not only these less known phenomena of mind but also describes that vast region of mental activity which takes place in the physical organism without our conscious thought as in the involuntary contraction and expansion of the lungs, the beating of the heart, the regulation of the circulation, digestion, the building up of the cells, and so on.[9]

---

[6] Jesus possessed these faculties. See Luke 7. Also my "Textbook of Psychology and Metaphysics," p. 26

[7] "The Great Secret" by Maeterlinck, p.245

[8] "Literature on psychoanalysis

[9] Students unfamiliar with this subject should by all means study my other publications, "The Law of Mind in Action,"

The most important fact of the subconsciousness is that all these mental processes take place without conscious thought. When we speak of "conscious thought" we refer to thinking in which the person is aware of himself as thinking, he is making choices, he is analyzing the subject, dissecting, debating, arguing, deciding, constructing hypotheses, rejecting as well as accepting ideas, etc. He is aware of himself as a thinker or a person. But the subconscious does not decide, and does not have the power to reject ideas. It takes whatever comes its way and if sufficiently impressed acts upon them. Like the soil of the earth to which we have likened it, it takes everything, rejects nothing, and grows the seed or word into the corresponding plant. To distinguish between the conscious and subconscious we often take the word personal to describe the former, and the word impersonal to describe the latter. It is all-important to our present subject to hold this distinction in mind. The subconscious mind of the individual and of society is impersonal. It is impressionable. It is plastic. It is open to suggestion. It is responsive. It is active. It is creative

---

"Faith That Heals," "Being and Becoming," and particularly "Textbook of Psychology and Metaphysics."

From the foregoing facts a law of mind may be easily formulated. This law, which is clearly set forth in my other books, must be briefly epitomized here as it is the basis of all "demonstration" either for healing bodies or businesses by mental means. It is as follows:

1. Mind is everywhere active throughout nature as subconscious intelligence

2. It is impersonal or receptive to all ideas

3. It is creative, as every idea is motorized, or put into action

4. The strongest idea rules

5. "Form" or result that is created is always like the idea which preceded it

Volumes could be written upon this one law. Unnumbered illustrations can be found both in the life of the reader and the society in which he finds himself

The knowledge and application of this law to healing will cure physical ills; to business and vocation, will bring success and financial freedom

In order to develop a sense of power and belief in the law, the student should make it a habit to observe its working in himself and environment; and should daily practice the principles here outlined

DAILY MEDITATION

I perceive in and around me the working of intelligence. I see that nothing happens by chance; and if it appears on the face that "it happened by luck," I shall search more deeply until I find the real facts in the case. I know that "whatsoever a man soweth, that shall he also reap." Today I shall enjoy the experience of deciding on the qualities I desire to have manifested in me and around me. I shall plant these ideas in the creative soil of the subconscious mind. I shall retain and believe only in that which means the big thing in my life. I shut out all opposing ideas. I expect a rich harvest. I am on the pathway which leads to success and nothing can stop me. I am success

CHART OF THE TWENTY SECRETS OF SUCCESS[10]	Percent
1. Physical Fitness and Personal Magnetism	
2. Mental Alertness	
3. Personal Appearance	
4. Originality	
5. Independence and Self-reliance	
6. Imagination	
7. Purpose	
8. Foresight	
9. Enthusiasm	
10. Self-control	
11. Will-power	
12. Obedience and loyalty	
13. Persistence	
14. Cheerfulness and Courage	
15. Good-will and Friendship	
16. Tact	
17. Bigness and Detail	
18. Knowledge of the Laws of Suggestion	
19. Work, Thrift, and Investment	
20. Moral Standards and Religious Faith	
Total	
Divide by 20 Equals Total Percent of Personal Efficiency	

[10] Figure each of these qualities on the basis of one hundred percent and then divide by twenty to get the average percent of your personal efficiency.

Chapter 8 SECRETS OF SUCCESS:
1. Physical Fitness and Personal Magnetism

A SUCCESSFUL soul requires a successful body. No life is worthwhile that is not enjoyed, and there is no fun in living with a body which is always making demands for consideration. The leg says, "I cannot go there." The eye says, "This light strains me and I won't work here." The head says, "I ache and I won't think." The liver rebels at sitting still, the arms rebel at moving. The stomach puts in a claim for damages, the heart murmurs, and the lungs wheeze. The kidneys command,

"Come along to the grave with me; I'm all worn out."

What is a poor man to do in the face of a situation like that? Even if he manages to "keep going," he has little chance of "getting there." Success demands the ability to "work overtime," "stand the strain," and remain magnetic at all times.

One should go definitely to work to recreate the body and develop personal magnetism. Our former books have given the method of treatment for physical healing, therefore we shall not discuss it here. But a word should be said about the creation of that over-plus of energy and physical fitness which we call "personal magnetism."

One of the great errors of the metaphysical systems of healing of our day lies in the disregard of the biological laws. It is said correctly that "matter is spirit at its lowest level," and then the fact is forgotten that there are laws of the lowest level as well as the highest. On the lowest level spirit is vibration, and form is built up by the groupings of electrical energies or corpuscles of electricity which we call electrons. In the body these energies are in a constant state of change, being cast off, consumed, and replaced every moment of time. The Originating Spirit may have brought energies into existence by the divine fiat or the Word, but having been brought into existence they are henceforth subject to the laws of their level. In the body new tissues are built up and wasted energies are replaced by the processes of nourishment, digestion, assimilation, osmosis, oxidation, and metabolism in the presence of the catalyzer which we call life or spirit. Without the life or spirit these processes do not take place. Without nourishment or oxygen, they cannot. Each is necessary to the other. The power of the Word (mental treatment) is the stimulation of these natural processes so that they take place harmoniously and rapidly. The body, from the physical point of view, therefore, is an electrical machine which uses energy and replaces it. It is a battery which must be constantly recharged, and when it is fully charged it is capable of remarkable magnetic vibration? When the body is so charged, it becomes a wonderful instrument for the ego or persona in the expression of personal magnetism.

The body is made up of sixteen primary elements, including oxygen, hydrogen, carbon, iron, magnesium, potassium, silicon, etc. These elements are being constantly consumed and must be replaced. They are taken into the system through the stomach, lungs, and skin. The ego or psyche presides over the processes by which they are converted into new energies, but it must have the material to work upon. It is necessary, therefore, to provide it.

1. Sane and careful attention should be paid to diet. By diet we do not refer merely to the popular misconception which thinks that it means half-starving oneself or eliminating everything one naturally likes. We mean scientific selection of proper foods and combinations of foods so as to provide the necessary elements for the replacement of those elements already consumed. No amount of mental treatment will permanently compensate for lack of proper nourishment, and those who desire the attainment of personal magnetism should learn the art of eating just as they would learn any other art. It is not our purpose here to teach dietetics. The student should turn to books already written on the subject.

We have known many great teachers of mental science who have disregarded this law of the lower level and have suffered the consequences in lessened vitality or even given up functioning on this level altogether. Intelligence or the spirit is all-powerful, and should be used in the selection of sane diet as well as in mental treatment. A large majority of persons may possibly be dietetically adjusted, that is, their food selections proper and well-balanced, in which case this word is not necessary for them. For those others who need it, however, too much emphasis cannot be placed upon the necessity of right eating.

In addition to the consideration of sane selection of foods, attention should be paid to simplicity (not more than four kinds at a meal), moderation (eating just enough and no more), water (to keep the system clean and replace the seventy percent of which the body is composed), and green or raw vegetables and fruits to maintain alkalinity. For general and popular purposes, the whole literature of vitamins may be boiled down into the statement that "cell salts" found in these foods are necessary to keep the body sweet, clean, and magnetic. The ordinary processes of the body produce acids which must be counteracted, balanced, and eliminated by alkalinity. The large part of diseases commonly called autointoxication, scorbutus, pellagra, scurvy, is really acidosis, and can be cured by the proper use of fruits and vegetables. A system overcharged with acidity cannot be magnetic. On the contrary, we find the person so afflicted expressing nervousness, depression, weariness unrelieved by rest, nerve tension, gloom, and other negative states. The whole "ignition system" is slowed up, the spark plugs are fouled, and there is neither brilliancy nor magnetism.

Summing it all up, then, the man or woman who desires to succeed must pay attention to what goes into and what goes out of the body.

2. Deep breathing is essential to the bodily processes.

After food is taken into the body it must be digested, and then passed through the appropriate channels to every cell of the organism. Meanwhile the blood picks up oxygen from the lungs and delivers it to the cell, where energy is created by the action of the oxygen upon carbon, just as we create heat or energy by burning coal in our furnaces.

It is a tragic fact that with a world full of oxygen, many are slowly dying for lack of breath.

Practice deep breathing. Learn to fill the lungs when breathing. It is not necessary to strain to do it. Simply watch yourself from time to time to see that you are getting the air. Don't economize on it. Occasionally breathe as deeply as you can and then hold the breath while you beat your chest all over with light blows.

Take brisk walks and breathe deeply all the way. Vary this by what has been termed "vitalic breathing." In this you take a partial breath on the first step, add to it on the second, and fill the lungs on the third. Then you exhale the whole on the fourth step. (One, inhale; two, inhale; three, inhale; four, exhale.) Vary this with two inhalations to one exhalation. Try it on running upstairs or practice by "still running" in your own room.

One who is much confined at his work and begins to feel nervous or depleted can overcome it immediately by right breathing and mental treatment. Sit down in an open chair with the arms hanging loose at the sides. Begin to lean forward, letting the head drop slowly by its own weight; then as far as you can, let each vertebra drop forward as though it were hinged on the one below it, until you have gradually let the whole upper body drop to the lowest point. While doing this you should exhale. Then slowly reverse while you inhale, until you are sitting upright once more. Do this three times. As you go down, state to yourself that you are dropping all your weariness and nervousness. As you come back, mentally affirm that you are filled with vitality and vigor.

One should be particularly careful on going to sleep to see that he is breathing deeply and to fix in his mind that he is going to breathe deeply all night long. It is unnecessary to state that one should sleep always with an open window, but just as important is the value of the open nose.

3. Personal magnetism is impossible in a weak muscular body. Out-of-door exercises are by far the most desirable, but good gymnasium work or bedroom calisthenics can be made to keep the system in tone, particularly if they be of the variety which exercises the abdominal part of the body as in the famous "daily dozen."

4. All these efforts to build up electrical energies will be of no avail if they are being constantly short-circuited. Many people continually ground their wires by unnecessary dissipation of energy, as in worry, uncertainty, apprehension, jerky movements, tapping the feet, drumming with the hands, fault-finding, chattering incessantly without thinking, "driving themselves," pressing (as they call it in golf), and so on.

Practice ease of movement, walk easily, talk easily, learn to be deliberate without being lazy, refuse to "be fussed," give up trying to "force" everything, look at things without staring at them. The last furnishes a good illustration of the difference between dissipating and retaining energy. Some sightseers go tensely from place to place. As Mary W. Montagu said in a letter to Mr. Pope,[11] "Everybody stares here; staring is a-la-mode—there is a stare of attention and interest, a stare of curiosity, a stare of expectation, a stare of surprise." Learn to allow impressions to flow in on you rather than to go out and seize them.

It is needless to say that energy can be conserved only as self-control is realized. Only the masterful mind can exercise a magnetic influence. It has often happened in history that men who have lacked physical vigor have compensated for it by the most positive quality of mind. You should determine to possess both. Emotional storms, jealousy, hatred, "hurt feelings," easy anger, vindictiveness or a desire to get even, brooding over wrongs or failures, all these and many other mental states cause the natural energies of the body to leak out, leaving the system demagnetized and thus a prey to mental, moral, and physical failure.

MENTAL TREATMENT

I know that I am possessed of a body capable of creating and storing powerful magnetic forces. Every day and hour I shall so act and think as to build up

---

[11] "Life and Letters," p. 138, Vol. II.

these forces. I am in the midst of the electrical energies of Nature and I shall draw upon her. Around me is the Vast Flowing Vigor of the Universe, all space is interpenetrated by the Vitality and Energy of Spirit. In It I live, move, and have my being, and Its strength is now become my strength, Its life is my life; every breath I breathe is the breath of the Spirit; I am radiant, happy, free, magnetic!

Chapter 9 SECRETS OF SUCCESS:
2. Mental Alertness

1. Interest 2. Ambition

SUCCESS involves interest in what one is doing. If you are not interested in your work, find out the reason at once. If it is not your kind of work, change as soon as possible. If it is your kind, then "snap into it" mentally. Interest means pleasure, keenness, alertness. It begets knowledge of one's goods, one's profession. It incites to observation. It leads to curiosity regarding the way others do the same work, to a desire to better methods, and excel in one's chosen field. Those who are mentally wide awake always have the advantage when it comes to advancement, because they have greater knowledge not only of their own department but of the business as a whole.

Walter C. Allen, President of the Yale and Towne Lock Company, who rose from truck boy to the head of a ten million dollar concern, once said in an interview:

"Too many of our young men have a fixed idea that opportunity must be thrust upon them, and at the same time do nothing to prepare themselves for grasping it when it comes. In spite of the fact that our company has refused to go outside for its officials and has promoted men from the ranks, we have had case after case where we actually tried to thrust promotion upon men who were apparently ambitious, but who had left themselves unprepared. Before the chance came, they complained because it was not handed to them on a silver tray, and when it did come they were unable to grasp it."

It can be seen from this how necessary it is to keep the interest in one's work alive. Those who have had no technical education can overcome their handicap in this way. The technique of most lines of business can be acquired by experience. Ofttimes the college graduate's advantage is merely in his trained powers of observation and thinking. Said Professor James in his famous chapter on Habit,[12] "Let no youth have any anxiety about the upshot of his education, whatever the line of it may be. If he keep faithfully busy each hour of the working day, he may safely leave the result to itself. He can with perfect certainty count on waking up some fine morning to find himself one of the competent ones of his generation, in whatever pursuit he may have singled out. Silently, between all the details of his business, the power of judging in all that class of matter will have built itself up within him as a possession that will never pass away. Young people

---

[12] "Psychology, Briefer Course," p. 150. By William James

should know this in advance. The ignorance of it has probably engendered more discouragement and faint-heartedness in youths embarking on arduous careers than all other causes put together."

Professor James is here seeking to remove the sense of strain with which so many face the problem of success. He is saying to us that the arts and thoughts of everyday experience in any field of effort will of themselves gradually build up our skill and knowledge and create the ability to take leadership in our particular field. But it must be borne in mind that we must not only act, we must think. Mental alertness is necessary.

Along with interest, I place ambition. I do not see how anyone can hope to succeed unless he is ambitious. He must have the forward look. His work today must have reference to tomorrow. Tomorrow and today must be one with him. His mind keeps on running after the clock has struck. It is twisting and turning around his work to find new ways, new solutions, new outlets. He is stimulated both by interest in the work itself and by his desire to succeed in that work.

Unhappy is he who has no ambition. To stultify ambition is to kill half the driving force of personality. The joy of the forward look! The pleasure of dreams! The thrill of anticipation! The more it means to you, the more meaning there is to life. True ambition robs no one, inspires the emulation of others, and opens the door to success.

TREATMENT

I possess the spirit of success. I am filled with interest and love for my work. I am mentally wide-awake. I have the vision to see new possibilities and new solutions, I observe carefully and remember perfectly. I am going ahead with confidence and courage, with purpose and determination.

The passion of attainment is upon me and I will succeed. I am success.

Chapter 10 SECRETS OF SUCCESS:
3. Personal Appearance

IT seems hardly necessary to comment upon the need of presenting a pleasing personal appearance. One takes this naturally for granted in our day. Yet I meet many whose failure has been hastened by neglect of dress, hair, hands, and powder-puff. A woman insurance agent in New York who is said to do the largest business of her kind of anyone of her sex in this country said that she owed her success to her powder-puff. She was using a figure of speech but we get the mental picture of a well-dressed, well-poised woman, unhurried, composed, unperspiring, and with the confidence that she is presenting an appearance of competence and success.

I knew a school principal who was slated for advancement to a very high post—until the trustees saw his feet! As far as I know, this man, with great learning, is still teaching a country high school because he does not know the value of personal appearance in the matter of shoestrings.

From the standpoint of sentiment, we can talk loudly of democracy and the license of genius. Practically we find the employer of labor and the patron of art alike making fatal appraisal of frayed coat sleeves, soiled nails, and bearded faces—male or female.

In the professional classes conducted by the author, it is a requirement that all students present themselves at the class dressed as well as they possibly can be for the occasion.

They must learn to acquire ease in the presence of others and this is impossible if one is unexpectedly singled out to say a few words from the platform, and finds himself conscious of his personal appearance.

The real art of dress for men consists in being clothed appropriately for the occasion and so that one's clothes are "taken for granted." No one would attempt to define the art for women.

Chapter 11 SECRETS OF SUCCESS:
4. Originality

ADVANCEMENT in any field means, of course, progress. If you wish to be advanced to a higher position, then you must contribute to the progress of the business. You cannot climb over dead business to a place on top. Many second class minds desire to get into a "soft seat" already prepared; but if you do not help to make a "job" you ought not to expect to hold it. There are very few lines of business or vocation today which will last until tomorrow unless changes are introduced into them. The law of business is in general the law of change. New methods of advertising, new ways of marketing, better this and better that must constantly be introduced. The great secret of progress is originality. Thousands of men and women owe their present success to their creative ability. They have seen the possibilities, have worked out the details, and increased the profits.

The vast economic advantage which America has over other countries is due not merely to our great natural resources, for other countries have enormous untapped sources of wealth, but to the inquisitive mind of our people, ever seeking new ways. This is especially true in the field of invention. America is said to excel all other countries put together in the number and variety of patents.

Invention means the harnessing of mechanical forces to do part or all of our work for us. Every man in America has an iron man working for him. We estimate the force of machinery at so many horse power, and billions of iron horses are working for us. But if we were to estimate the saving of labor effected by machinery; appliances; methods of filing, teaching, etc., we would find that millions of iron men are working for us. These iron men wear out but it costs but little to feed, clothe, and educate them, and nothing for luxuries!

Originality and the spirit of invention, then, are in themselves sources of wealth, and it is this that has helped to make America great, for she has drawn not only upon her native sons and daughters for genius, but has stripped the world of its most daring and original minds, and casting them all into the melting pot has brought forth still greater masters of invention and industry. And we are just at the beginning of what is to be! A new world is before us, not merely a world of mechanics, but a world of method, of efficiency, of art, and music, of song and dance—of things hidden from the foundations of the earth, which the minds of today and tomorrow will conceive and bring forth. The great age of applied psychology is at hand. This is unequivocally voiced by the noted author, H. G. Wells, and many other modern seers.

Can anything be plainer? You are "to use your head." The only way to get ahead is to use it. Keep on the lookout for the better way in everything.

Casson in his book on "Ads and Sales" has this to say, "When Howe put the eye of the needle in the point of the needle, he found a better way. When McCormick hitched a team of horses to a reciprocating scythe, he found a better way. When Mergenthaler created a machine by means of which type can be made instead of set, he found a better way. . . . What we may expect in the near future is a period of inventive-ness, better ways of doing the same old thing."

Russell Conwell, that grand old man whose mind was "Acres of Diamonds," whose voice inspired millions to believe in themselves, to dare to be original and individual, tells many tales of the outcome of such daring.

Success does not demand that every man and woman shall be an inventor but it requires originality. I have always loved the story of the young woman who attended a meeting of some Daughters of the American Revolution each of whom claimed to be the descendant of a general or at least a colonel. Parading up and down with a very grand air, she affected the utmost snobbery until the inquiry was made as to what noted ancestor had given her the right to such superiority. Finally someone asked her the direct question, to which she replied, "I am descended from the only private in the American Revolution."

No people in the world are so prone to "joke" as Americans for we love the original turn of mind that creates it. Let us therefore not fail to develop the faculty of originality. Keep the mind open to new ways. Study your personality, vocation, and business, to see what new and better elements you may introduce. And if you lack the necessary instinct, create it by proper suggestion.

SUGGESTION

My mind is open and receptive to new ideas. I am observant and I understand the principles upon which my business or vocation is established. New solutions will present themselves to me. I can and will add to my own efficiency and that of others with whom I am associated. I have the spirit of originality and invention. I enjoy the study and the solution of problems. I am one-hundred percent wide awake.

Chapter 12 SECRETS OF SUCCESS:
5. Independence and Self-Reliance

SUCCESS sooner or later involves leadership. It means taking a place where you must do the primary thinking. You may be guided by the policy of the firm, by tradition and habit, but there will come times when you must think and decide. Many lose their nerve at this point. They have not cultivated self-reliance.

The psycho-analyst knows that many people are sufferers from a curious neurosis, the necessity of leaning on someone else. There is a period in child life when it is natural to depend upon the mother and father and be guided by their word and wisdom. But at the age of puberty the natural transition is made from their authority to one's own. Sometimes the father is too dominant and exercises his own will at the expense of the developing will of the child. He keeps the boy in subjection until he relies entirely upon the father. Sometimes the mother says, "My boy has only one sweetheart—his mother. He would rather be with me than anyone else." Or, "My girl never thinks of going out without me." This attitude leads to the eventual loss of mental independence on the part of the new generation, for even after parents die or the child marries, the sense of dependence is transferred to the husband, wife, or someone else.

To overcome this condition is no easy task. The ambitious man or woman who lacks self-reliance should begin at once to develop it. Every necessary step should be taken, but above all there should be mental treatment and practice. Give yourself constructive suggestions every day. Affirm your mental independence and your faith in your own powers and judgment. Affirm that you are capable of leadership, that you believe in yourself and in your own judgment. Go out then and try to do and act in accordance with your affirmation.

Nothing is more important than to act definitely on every resolution or affirmation. The subconscious mind will then retain the impression and begin to build up the actual state. You say, "I am self-reliant, I have the spirit of leadership, I am decisive and ready to assume responsibility," then act as though this is true whether it is true for the moment or not. Presently you will find it easier and easier to believe in your independence and consequently to act with forceful self-reliance.

Chapter 13 SECRETS OF SUCCESS:
6. Imagination

THE story of big business is the story of imagination. Every factory sings the saga of a dream; every whirling wheel of the Transcontinental beats it out measure by measure. You can hear it in the staccato of the riveting hammer; your own motor hums it; and far above your head it is intoned in the swift processional of the winged plane. The great romances of America will be written around the adventures of industry. Harriman dreamed a railroad across the continent, holding pencil and paper in hand and tracing imaginary lines. Langley watching the flight of the birds caught the ghostly outlines of the heavier-than-air machine that was later to sweep the sky. Carnegie and Gary, each in his way, spun the steel fabric that dramatizes American progress. The rise and fall of markets, the inflow and outflow of merchandise, the flame of passion that lights a nation to arms and the flicker as it dies in the cold morning of victory — these, too, were once "only a thought." All progress, all invention, all machinery, all organization, are the crystallization of dreams.

Let men talk, if they will, about "the hard-headed business man." But he is neither wood nor ivory, and, contrary to popular opinion, he does not have glass eyes. Over the hot metal of his mind there hovers the blue light of creative thought. He is a leader, a master, a power, because he had the imagination to assemble all the intricate parts of the great machine of industry. He had to formulate the plan that causes a thousand unrelated pieces, forces, mechanics, laborers, artisans, architects, to become as one, to act and react harmoniously each on the other to some great end. Practical, dynamic, ruthless, it may be, but not unimaginative. The bridge that spans the torrent, the tunnel that pierces the vitals of the earth, the structure that outvies the Tower of Babel, are human dreams come true.

It was reported in the press that Edison on his seventy-first birthday declared that one of the qualities of success which is vital to the young men of today is imagination. It must be cultivated. Arthur E. Stilwell, who built more miles of railroad than any man living today, told me that all he ever did was the outcome of a mental picture which was presented to him so clearly as to have all the apparent reality of having been created and sketched by another mind. His imagination was like a die stamping its imprint upon the responsive surface of his practical mind. It was like the intelligence department of an army, for it ran ahead of the rails and spotted out difficulties to be avoided and advantages to be won.

The unimaginative mind cannot hope to see the good which lies ahead to encourage him nor the bad to be avoided. When the day of disaster is upon him, he wonders at his "hard luck" or blames an "Inscrutable Providence," not knowing that his own lack of imagination is scrutable improvidence.

The first quality of creation in any line is imagination. Imagination is the model, the plan, the sketch, the aim, the goal, the dramatized idea, the concept without which the form itself can never appear. The image is necessary to the actual. God himself cannot be conceived as having created without first having a mental picture of the thing to be created. There are no "things" from which the Originating Mind can pattern. The idea must exist first. The thought becomes the thing, but it must first be thought. For every phenomenon there must be a noumenon. The germ in the seed, the life-principle in the egg, the soul in the body, determines the form into which it will develop. What you will have will be determined by what you will to have. Imagination is not will but it is the sine qua non, of will. You cannot will unless you have something about which to will.

Imagination is a time-saver, a labor-saver, a trouble-saver. It prevents wasted effort, it hews to a line, and it marches to a goal. It has a way of getting things done which astonishes us. We had thought the thing insurmountable until some master came along and inspired the worker with his dream. Suddenly the end appeared like magic.

Imagination has a way of working out its own problems. We can better understand this if we will recall what we said in an earlier chapter about the subconscious mind. We there found that the subconscious is creative, tending to work out the details of all plans submitted to it; creating a diseased form for those who hold a diseased thought; bringing health to those who impress the idea of health upon it. The body is subject to habit. Repeated action and thought create definite reflexes. What you believe, you begin to do; what you continue to do, you eventually find yourself doing automatically. This is why we are told in the Scripture to "guard our thoughts." And again, "Keep thy heart (thoughts and emotions) with all diligence, for out of it are the issues of life."

One of the most interesting experiments of which I have known was one performed by the well-known practical psychologist, Dr. William F. Kelley. He one day determined to impress his subconscious forces with the idea of the automatic movement of some part of his body to show that one direct impression planted at the psychological moment will produce permanent results. He accordingly placed himself in a self-induced subconscious state and affirmed that his thumb would automatically swing from the joint and go on "waggling" in this way indefinitely and without his conscious control. After "planting the suggestion," he brought himself back to normal consciousness, and began observation of the thumb. He found that the action was autonomic and the reflex as definite as though acquired by long practice. No amount of conscious effort or command was sufficient to control the movement. The subconscious mind had accepted the idea and continued to carry it out. He tells very amusingly of the unexpected call of a friend at this moment and how "for two hours I held my waggling thumb behind my back in the greatest state of uneasiness as I was not prepared to pronounce my experiment a success until I was sure I could safely conclude it by stopping the wiggly thing!"

Having later on secured the time necessary for specific concentration, he became sufficiently subjective to reimpress the subconscious with the desired mental image, upon which the movement ceased.

"This is a graphic illustration of the creative power of imagination. It shows why a belief begets the thing believed; why disease is, as Mrs. Eddy says, "An image of thought held in the mind until it appears on the body." Failure is a mental image crystallized into form.

There are those who are always declaring that they expect to fail; that they never have any luck; that the other fellow always gets ahead. And they reap as they sow.

On the other hand, we see men and women excelling in every walk of life because they excel in the powers of imagination. Hear what Nurmi, the great mercurial marvel, claims is the secret of his success: "Muscles—a piece of rubber!" he cries scornfully.

"Muscles are nothing. Mind is everything. An athlete is the product of the crystallization of his mind and his muscle is the visualized form of his will-power and intelligence.

"All I have achieved is due to my spiritual, not physical faculties. Body is merely the instrument on which the mind plays,"

The great runner insists that many of his rivals have had better muscles than he. "But there was a spiritual spark," he adds, "that gave me superiority. A great pianist's magic does not lie in the muscularity of his fingers, or in practice, or even in his technical knowledge, but in a spiritual something which no one can account for. I consider everything that I have achieved due to my mental faculties."

Diet, he maintains, is only of secondary importance in a runner's success. "As a rule," he says, "a milk and vegetable diet and a generally healthy way of living are essentials. But there are no material secrets which make one man superior to another." I say that no man ever dreamed too high and lofty a dream.

I say that no man ever soared the heavens who feared to leave the ground. Let your mind run before you to plan great things. In the words of Angela Morgan:

> *"I will hew great windows for my soul,*
> *Channels of splendor, portal of release;*
> *Out of earth's prison walls will I hew them,*
> *Through stratus of human strife and passion,*
> *I will tunnel a way, I will carve and fashion,*
> *With the might of my soul's intensity,*
> *Towering out of Time.*
> *I will breathe the air of another clime,*
> *That my spirit's pain may cease.*
> *That the being of me have room to grow,*
> *That my eyes may meet God's eyes and know,*
> *I will hew great windows, wonderful windows,*
> *Measureless window, for my soul.*[13]

---

[13] "Room," from "The Hour Has Struck," by Angela Morgan. Dodd, Mead and Company.

Let others warn you of impracticality. Let others tell you "to be sensible and not to expect too much." Let them advise you of the necessity of keeping well within the bounds of reasonable expectancy. Let them prate of dreams unfulfilled and hopes deferred; let them return to their wonted toil, but I shall tell you only to believe. Believe in yourself, believe in your dream, believe in the power within and around you that takes your thought into the inner recesses of its own being, and in the secret chambers of creation weaves and chisels, molds and makes, or "grows ye know not how," that which your soul demands.

TREATMENT

This treatment should be begun with the assurance to yourself that you are aware that there is within you a virgin power capable of becoming anything you may desire. All new ideas must start somewhere. The possibility of the rise of a new idea is just as great in you as in anyone else. These ideas will rise when an outlet has been provided. This outlet is the mental attitude of expectancy along the given line, whether it be new plots for stories, new concepts for art, new motives for music, new inventions, new ways in business. Give the mind free play for imagination. Assert that new ideas are coming to you, and that they are coming of their own accord without strain of any kind. Assert that your imagination is all-creative, that you are open and receptive to all constructive impressions, and that you will receive them. Learn to look for these impressions and to be quick to seize upon the ideas that rise in consciousness. A very little thread will lead to a very great discovery. "I am receptive to the slightest impulse of Creative Spirit. New ideas swarm to the windows of my mind begging for admission. I believe in my own ideas and will hold to those which impress me as worthwhile in spite of any objections. I will work to their acceptance and they will be accepted."

Chapter 14 SECRETS OF SUCCESS:
7 Purpose

I CANNOT believe that life is just one thing after another; this happening because that has happened, and something else going to happen because this is happening. For the purposes of psychology it is said that we do not need to posit a soul; that consciousness is merely the activity of one cell upon another and the passage of impressions from new cells to old, and these growing dimmer and dimmer until they ebb out into the sea of forgetfulness. Account for life in whatever way you will, the fact remains there is "That- In-Us" which not only accepts the impressions that impinge upon us from without and cognizes cell movements within, but also has the ability to choose the nature of its own reaction. It is not the product of its environment but it adjusts itself to its environment in order to survive and to become master in it. This is the real meaning of "adaptiveness." Moreover, "the soul" has the power of initiating vibration, movement, and change. It can become the causa causans to a whole new stream of impressions and movements. To believe otherwise is to settle into the hopeless waters of Karma and to spin like a dead leaf on the circle of a whirlpool, and you may not escape because you are always having experiences which grow out of the past and which bind you to an inevitable future.

On the other hand, to give to the soul the power of initiation, and to endow it with purpose is to rise on the wings of a bird and settle on other and more favorable waters of experience.

Herein is man's glory that he is a self-conscious entity with the power of purpose. He can have a goal. He can select an objective. He can decide on a new plan entirely unconnected with past experience and leading into other paths than anything in his former setting could have promised. Witness the glorious rebirth of "Twice Born Men,"[14] "Other Sheep,"[15] and "Varieties of Religious Experience."[16] Rebirth is a psychological change, it is a reversal of a man's mental outlook, but it is also a metaphysical change for it means the awakening of the soul to the higher purposes for which it has come into the world. Shall we hesitate to say, in the light of religious experiences like these, that the soul has come into this world with an aim and a goal, and that a definite purpose engages the incarnating consciousness? Certain it is that the Bible and other holy books and teachings of the past lead us to this assumption; and modern psychology gives us corroborative evidence.

---

[14] 1 and 2
[15] Harold Begbie.
[16] James

The study of certain types of sickness under the light of psychoanalysis reveals the fact that many men and women are suffering from psychic disturbances which denote that the personality itself is out of harmony with its environment. Many forms of neurosis are due to a "sick psyche," but the psyche is sick because it is not satisfied with what it is doing. It came to fulfill a different destiny. It is here to work out other problems. It is seeking experiences at another angle. And when its purpose is thwarted it feels dissatisfied, it is determined to "be free or no longer be." It shakes the body like the tremor of an earthquake, it stabs it with pain, it poisons it with acids, it struggles like a mad thing, and either converts the mind to new issues or withdraws altogether.

The successful psychoanalyst probes the consciousness to find the hidden psychic causes of these physical agitations. He goes back into the history of the patient, he analyzes all his repressed emotions, buried memories, unconscious likes and dislikes, and over and over again, he discovers that the sickness is none other than the failure of the psyche to fulfil itself.[17]

---

[17] See "The Great Secret" by Maeterlinck, p. 234, showing the experiments of De Rochas

Success therefore can never be fully attained unless we find the purpose which animates our existence. Herein lies the value of vocational psychology that it helps to discover the special genius with which we are endowed and which we are here to express.[18]

Moreover, as the success of our life here upon the earth is to be determined by the extent to which we fulfill our destiny, so is it true of individual undertakings. It is not an undertaking unless it is a purpose. If it is a purpose, it is a destiny. The star of destiny is indeed the star of purpose, for as we proceed to the purpose we fulfill the destiny. We are our destiny; for if we are progressing toward our goal in a definite and purposeful way, we are at each moment just where we ought to be at that moment; and thus we do not have to wait to get our reward for that is ever with us as we look complacently upon our present situation as the complete fulfillment of destiny up to this point, It is the selection of a purpose that marks the man! No kind or unkind fate marks him, nor man more unkind! He marks himself. Because of his steadfast purpose he lives a different kind of life from others. His attention is on the positive rather than the negative. He worries

---

[18] See Chap. VI, Vol. II, of this Series, "How to Choose a Career."

less, he ignores more. He is calmer in peril, steadier in suspense, firmer in faith, and philosophic in doubt.

I believe that life has meaning only as it has purpose. It is anticipation that gives us wings to rise above the discouragements and staleness of the present hour. Today's reward is often only tomorrow's gain. Today can be lived because of tomorrow's goal.

> *"For acts in hours of insight willed,*
> *May be through hours of gloom fulfilled.*
> *Not 'til the hours of light return.*
> *All we have reaped can we discern."*

Definiteness of goal is above all to be desired. Says Bulwer Lytton:

> *"He who seeks one thing in life, and but one,*
> *May hope to achieve it before live is done:*
> *But he who seeks all things, wherever he goes.*
> *Only reaps in the hopes which around him he sows.*
> *A harvest of barren regrets: And the worm*
> *That crawls on in the dust to the definite term*
> *Of his creeping existence, and sees nothing more*
> *Than the half-sage, whose course, fixed by no friendly star,*
> *Is by each star distracted in turn, and who knows.*
> *Each will still be as distant, wherever he goes."*

Chapter 15 SECRETS OF SUCCESS: 8. Foresight

How many there are who are "stumbling" into trouble, into sorrow, and failure, because they do not "look before they leap!" Success requires foresight. It demands a careful survey of the field before entering upon it. The unforeseen circumstances may be the deciding factor in the enterprise, and while you may not know in advance all that is going to happen, you can know what may happen, and make provision for it.

Foresight is a combination of imagination and judgment. The imagination runs ahead and spies out the land. It pictures all the processes of the undertaking. It penetrates walls and windows, makes long journeys, visits inner offices of banks and businesses, enters other minds and reads their secret? You can mentally go where you want to go and look over every factor in the case with the eye of imagination. Then having seized upon these factors you can array them before reason and have judgment passed upon them.

The foresight of many business men is almost like prescience. They seem to know in advance. The accuracy of their forecasts is startlingly correct.

What man may know about coming events has always been the subject of discussion. The clergy have argued it pro and con. They have exalted or damned prophecy according to their bias, but no one can deny that "coining events cast their shadows before."

The difference between a forecast and intuition should be noted. One could write a whole book on "hunches" telling of the remarkable forecasts of events in business and markets. I personally knew a woman who followed a profession, but had a distinct gift in regard to "markets," a direct intuition. She would call her broker and place her orders to buy with such definiteness and success as to indicate an almost direct knowledge of what the market would do. In this way she amassed a considerable fortune. But after she had succeeded in making herself financially independent, she decided to go down on the market herself. So she gave up her professional work and became a speculator. But now her situation was entirely different. She was in the midst of rumors, intrigues, "tips," deceits, and all the chaotic mental atmosphere of the market where her intuitive powers were constantly clouded with faulty suggestions. She found her "hunches" no longer dependable, and in a few swift weeks her money was swept away on the tide of speculation.

In this case we can see the activity of pure intuition, but I would not call this foresight. It was not so much a matter of making a mental picture as it was of allowing her mind to receive mental impressions, upon which she took definite action. Business foresight might include this intuitive power, but it also includes knowledge of the various factors in the case. It is an open secret that many of the large operators of this country are constant visitors upon "psychics." These psychics have a peculiar faculty of "sensing" subtle mental impressions which have not yet become vivid enough to become consciously recognized. There are ideas which are still "in solution," but which are soon to crystallize. Often the psychic can "get" these. The difficulty comes of course in being able to discriminate between the impressions. There is always a great mass of ideas in solution; ideas both good and bad, some of which will materialize and some which will not. For this reason we could not recommend the practice which we mention. In fact, we would warn against it, for the simple reason that the vast majority who search out these psychics do not have the discrimination which passes judgment upon the impressions presented. On the other hand, great financiers whose names we might mention have found it of value to get these impressions and then to go ahead with a wide knowledge of actual conditions and a well-balanced judgment, to carry out their plans. These plans may mean the manipulation of the market with the full knowledge of the stock to be manipulated. They know the assets of the company back of it, the liabilities, the management, the present market for the product, etc., etc. Coupling their "hunch," their imagination, their reason, they take definite action with the result that the bigger operators usually succeed.

Of course what is true on the market is doubly true in the world of legitimate business. We will suppose that a woman is going into the millinery business. She must first have a location. There must be materials to work with. There must be a reasonably certain market. But this is not enough. There must be the most divine imagination. Not only must each hat itself be a work of art, a "creation" different from every other hat on earth, that has been, is, or is to be; but she must also know in advance that this hat which she is about to make will be the kind of hat that some woman will want, not now but perhaps three months from now, when the season is on. Future styles! Knowledge of what women are wearing today will not be enough. What will they want tomorrow? They don't know yet, but she must! Will the brims be wide or narrow? Will the crowns be high or low? Will the material be felt or straw, or both, or neither? Will the basket contain flowers or fruit?

Even if success does not hang by a thread, it certainly is often hung by a ribbon.

Ninety-five percent of new businesses in this country are said to fail, and one of the chief reasons is the lack of foresight and the failure or inability to "read the signs of the times," and prepare in advance not only for normal requirements, abnormal emergencies, and so on but even for psychologies. This is well illustrated in the case of a merchant friend of mine. He conducted a store in a small Ohio town and dealt in women's cloaks and dresses. He did his buying in New York and in his early years used to go to the city periodically to purchase what he considered the latest and best thing. He would lay in a supply of dresses ranging from seventy-five to a hundred dollars and bring them triumphantly home expecting them to be "snapped up." But woman after woman would come to the store, look at a dress, feel it, and pass on. Without any reason but with a uniformity of psychology which baffles analysis, the women of the town would "turn down" what he had expected they would "snap up," and the dresses would go onto the bargain counter at fifteen dollars apiece. From this experience he learned to bring home only two or three dresses and watch the first women who examined them. If they bought he put in a big order for more. If they "passed them up," he did not order more.

THE CASE OF ARTHUR E. STILWELL

In studying the problem of business foresight, I have been very much interested in the career of Arthur E. Stilwell, the railroad builder.[19] It has been my good fortune to know him personally for a number of years and to discuss these things with him. He has always exercised a remarkable psychic power which doubtless all possess but which few have developed. From his earliest youth, he was able to penetrate the world of mental causes with such accuracy as to constitute a virtual prophetic power. Mental convictions would come to him with such definiteness as to lead him to act upon them often against the judgment of his associates but with ultimate success. The most interesting incident occurred in connection with the building of the Kansas City and Southern Railroad. Those acquainted with this road know that it ends in the south at Port Arthur, the greatest land-locked harbor of its kind. This location for the terminal was not the one selected by engineers, who preferred Galveston, but was used by the insistence of Mr. Stilwell whose faculties of intuition and judgment led him to forecast the very disaster which afterwards overtook Galveston. Port Arthur was completed just as

---

[19] He has built more miles of railroad than any man living today.

the tidal wave struck the Texas city, and had the terminal been placed there it would have been swept away.

Whatever explanation we may give to this almost prophetic faculty, we must at least recognize the fact that there are remarkable powers within us, which can be utilized to bring success, and to provide against the failures which overtake those who do not utilize them. One might bear with stoic calm the vicissitudes of fortune, but who can endure the failure which is due entirely to the neglect of that which might have been foreseen and forestalled?

Scientific use of the laws of the subconscious will save us from such tragic mistakes. We must bear in mind that the subconscious is in touch with a wide field of facts of which the conscious mind may at the present moment be ignorant. It remembers important points which the conscious phase of mind has forgotten; it is the recipient of impressions from other minds; it has observed numerous details which escaped conscious attention.

In short, the facts are ready for an interpretation. This interpretation may take the nature of prophecy.

It is in identically the same way that discoveries of science are constantly being made. The facts are observed, it is perceived that there is some relationship between these facts, this relationship is found to be of an orderly kind; and so an hypothesis is drawn up proclaiming other facts which must naturally flow from those already known. It was in this way that the planet Neptune was discovered. No human eye had ever seen it, but in studying the movement of the planet Uranus through space it was found that the latter had the habit of running off the orbit it was naturally supposed to follow. From the observation of these facts the hypothesis was established that there must be another and unknown planet somewhere off in space which was exercising an influence upon it. It remained for a young mathematician to compute the orbit of the unknown and hypothetical planet. After two years of herculean mental effort John Sharpe Williams plotted the point in space, the telescope was trained upon it, and Neptune was discovered.

Such use of the mind bears the nature of prophecy and the forecast of coming events is by no means out of the reach of those who will use their mental forces scientifically,[20]

---

[20] Remanding prophetic functions of the mind, it will be interesting for the student to note the studies made by

Guidance of the mental forces should, therefore, be carefully sought in order that gross errors may not be made.

In general practice it is only necessary to follow these steps:

1. Take time to use your mental forces for the purpose at hand. Too many act first and think afterwards. There is no brilliancy in thinking afterwards of the clever things you might have said or done.

2. Carefully look over all the facts at hand. Get your working data—everything that pertains to the matter in hand.

3. Review the powers of mind and renew your faith in them asserting your ability to pass sensible judgment upon these facts and to come to a reasonable and correct solution.

4. State definitely that your mind now knows the steps you should take and will guide you in what you should do. Dwell upon this at some length until you feel that this knowledge is fully developed within you.

Flammarion in his book, "Death and Its Mystery," Vol. II, "At the Point of Death."

5. Assert that you will be able to go confidently forward and that you will not make mistakes in the choices you will be called upon to make from time to time.

6. Go to work.

How necessary it is that we awaken our hidden and sleeping forces. Cultivate imagination! Practice planning! Make mental surveys! Develop judgment! Look to the future! Soon you will find yourself exercising an "uncanny" power which will amaze others by the accuracy of its forecasts.

> *"The lightning-bug is brilliant,*
> *But it hasn't any mind;*
> *It stumbles through existence,*
> *With it headlight on behind."*

Which way is your headlight pointed?

Chapter 16 SECRETS OF SUCCESS:
9. Enthusiasm

HAPPY is the man whose work is his greatest hobby! It is then that work becomes play and business or vocation is one great game. Then he regrets to see the day close, and the morning dawns with a new delight. New plans to make! New paths to follow! New adventures! And old familiar things! The pleasant routine, friends and associates, smell of paints and oils, hum of wheels, buzz of voices, movement, action, persuasive speech, creative effort, a career in full swing! In such a situation enthusiasm is natural. The body-cells are alive, they are intoxicated, energy bubbles over.

And who can resist the appeal of such a personality! Enthusiasm is contagious, it lights up the interest, it inflames the imagination, it fires desire. It casts its spell upon all. Then they see with your eyes, they believe as you believe, and they want to do what you want them to do.

Enthusiasm does not mean ignorance and it does not mean bluff or deceit. The spell of enthusiasm can be woven successfully only by those who know what they are talking about, and believe in it. One who genuinely loves his work comes to know it thoroughly. He reads, studies, talks, dreams, about it. He knows the ins and the outs, the forward and back of his subject. If he is a salesman, he knows the location of his goods, the quantity on hand, the quality or kind, the purpose or use, the constituent elements or parts, the make or construction, the design or style, the finish or effect, the history or sentimental value, the price and the terms. When a customer comes he does not have "to hunt something up." He does not "aim to please"; he shoots.

For comparative purposes let us look at the uninterested and uninteresting salesman. A customer wants a trunk. The clerk will "see if we can find what you want. Our stock is low. Here is one. It is an awfully handy wardrobe trunk. It is awful good. It is awfully well finished. It is awful cheap."

The customer comes to the natural conclusion that it is an awful trunk. People like to be waited on by one who knows. They may have only an indefinite idea of what they want and they like to be told the various points, so that they may choose intelligently. Only one who has information can impart it. Only those who love their work acquire the necessary flare.

I shall never forget my early experiences as a salesman. I began in my teens as a house-to-house canvasser for stereoscopes. This instrument, unknown to the present generation, was one of the seven wonders of the world.

It was a domestic brother of the stereopticon which in turn was the forerunner of the moving-picture machine. It was like a huge pair of goggles, with magnifying lenses, mounted on a thin strip of wood which acted as a carrier for a slide in front of it. Into this slide you slipped a piece of cardboard on which were mounted two identical pictures. When looking through the lenses with a proper focus these two pictures blended into one giving depth or perspective, or what we call the third dimension. Thus to look at a picture of the Alps was like looking at real mountain scenery. The background had life, and color, and meaning.

Many people in those days kept cabinets for their pictures as we keep phonograph records today. One could open a box and bring forth a trip to Italy, or China, or California. One could see the great celebrities of the times, all dressed up ready to do something to celebrate them.

Armed with samples, I toured the rurals of New Hampshire, bent on a mission of enlightenment, the high priest of art and the advocate of foreign travel by proxy. Cook's tours could not have presented a more enthusiastic representative or one more widely traveled—by proxy. Was it not I whose

"---soul today is far away
Sailing the Vesuvian Bay.
My winged boat a bird afloat
Swims round the purple peaks remote."

Had not I with my own eyes looked upon Mont Blanc—

"Thou too, hoar Mount, thou that as I
raise my head
Awhile bowed low in adoration,
Upward from thy base slow traveling
With dim eyes suffused with tears,
Solemnly seems like a vapory cloud to rise
before me.
Rise, O ever rise!"

And how it rose! While my trembling and eager fingers placed it in the slide before the astonished eyes of a new traveler into parts unknown. Could anyone resist such journeys, such peeps into forbidden cities, such intimate contact with the great of the world? What neighbor could boast of such wide itineraries! Here in your own home you are cosmopolite, adventurer, critic of art, connoisseur of valuable and historic collections!

No, they could not resist it! And their collections swelled to bigger and ever bigger proportions as they added Africa, Australia and America to the wonders of

Europe and Asia, under the persuasive enthusiasm of a world-traveler by proxy.

So I have come to stress the value of enthusiasm, begotten of truth. You may be sure that what you value someone else will value. What is intriguing to you will be intriguing to another.

The world is richer, too, for your enthusiasms. Your employer's interest is aroused. You become a personality. You are somebody! To know your subject, even if it be but the points of a domestic rug, or a new nipple for the baby's bottle, or how pins are manufactured, is to become a raconteur—and all the world loves a story.

It is said that "all the world loves a lover." I shall not say less for him who loves his work, his task, his opportunity. The world needs faith. It needs the inspiration of those who believe in what they are doing and think that life is worthwhile.

If you lack enthusiasm you can begin today a definite cultivation of the qualities which inspire it. You can affirm your interest, your joy. You can daily increase your happiness by giving yourself the constructive suggestions which will create it. "I am happy. I am filled with the joy of my work. I have a fine sense of values and the spirit of an enthusiast."

Chapter 17 SECRETS OF SUCCESS: 10. Self-Control

IT is not control of the self we should seek but control by the self. We have already seen how many there are whose self is controlled by the emotions, by the senses, by bodily ailments. It is bound in chains by its own creation and led into miserable captivity. To one who has broken the bonds and come to live in the freedom of the self, it seems as though there never could have been a time when any other state was thought desirable. Yet we find many who think that self-control will mean merely self-denial, restraint, a lackluster life. They feel that as they live in a world of sensational experience, they will suffer loss if they can no longer be swayed by the appetites of the flesh, the passions of love and resentment. But control by the self does not mean self-denial. On the contrary, it means self-satisfaction; that is, the satisfaction which the self feels and should feel in its own dominance and priority.

To one who exults in conquest and the spirit of it, what greater appeal can there be than in the high adventure of self-mastery? Here is no mean battle, for it is a battle in which the forces of sense, myriad in number, are pitted against the self. The most thrilling story of this struggle that was ever told is that of the Bhagavad Gita. That majestic tale is understood only as we recognize

Arjuna as the "self," the ego or spirit, going into battle against the forces of the physical nature.

This is not the ascetic destruction of the natural emotions of the physical life, but merely the story of the ascendency of the spirit within and the necessity of self-control, or control by the self.

While lecturing in Morosco Theatre in New York some years ago, I was approached by a young man who told me, a propos of some illustrations I had been giving, how he had a short time before become very angry with another man. He had spoken heatedly and furiously. Suddenly his face froze into a distorted and disagreeable posture, and it was a week before he could control the muscles and bring the expression to normal.

Possibly the golf course affords as good an object lesson in the futility of the indulgence of the passions as any place on earth, because after all it is a game, and one would not look to see men take themselves so seriously in a game. Yet I have seen them pound the ground with their clubs, throw their clubs after their ball, throw their balls after the club, seize the club and bend it around a convenient tree, swear like the seven demons, fall into a silent rage from which they would not emerge for the balance of the game.

In the old days when a man's muscle was the self-starter of a Ford, I have seen men kick the car because the engine would not start.

But one need not extend the illustrations. The reader will possibly be able to add some of his own. The great necessity is to establish the procedure for self-control.

In cultivating self-control by the use of mental laws, it should be borne in mind that the subconscious is neutral or impersonal. It is a "good" mind and a "bad" one according to the nature of the dominant mental impression or the ruling ideas and ideals of the personality. Conversion, as we have seen, merely means the withdrawal of old mental pictures, ideals, and aspirations, and the substitution of newer and higher ones. Even as the soil of Mother Earth does not protest if we uproot the weeds and plant lilies, so the subconscious mind makes no protest when we change the seed of thought and plant nobler and finer words and ideas. The subconscious becomes to us what we become to it.

Accordingly we should put our minds on the highest and best things. We must shut our eyes from looking on those things which create faulty mental pictures and suggestions. We should be constantly on the lookout for that which will help and upbuild. We see in this world just about what we are looking for. If we are looking for the bad, we shall see it. If for the good, there is always some to find.

A teacher in one of our public schools told the children to bring a picture to school with something in it representing "light." A little fellow from the East Side brought a card portraying a filthy and indecent scene. The teacher looked at it with disgust. "How dare you bring that filthy thing here?" "Why, teacher," said the boy with tears streaming down his cheeks, "don't you see de moon, shinin' in de winder?" And sure enough there was the crescent moon sending its pure, white ray through the dirty pane and into the mind of the child who saw it because he was looking for it.

The cultivation of self-control is largely a matter of controlling the direction of our attention. Those whose passions are easily aroused cannot afford to listen to "suggestive plays," or look at sensuous pictures, or yield to "seductive music with its sensuous decoy.[21] Nor can they afford companionship which exercises negative suggestions.

---

[21] Note, p. 74, in the author's "Songs of the Silence."

The mind must be placed "on higher things." Every effort should be made toward the environment of cultivated influences, literature, and associations.

It is wise to make it a daily habit to read the teachings of Jesus in the New Testament, or the fine, inspiring books of the "New Philosophy." Wiser still to take time each day and mentally picture oneself in the setting of mental and spiritual refinement. See yourself ideally. Dream yourself into nobility. Seat yourself on a throne — the throne of the House of David. Fill the mind with the picture of yourself as you really are, a master of life, a master of the passions — the self in all its divine nobility in ascension. Mentally create the concept of that high spiritual self you are as a real person, clothed in the regal garments which become one who, though he has traveled far, still is an honored son in his father's house.

Chapter 18 SECRETS OF SUCCESS:
11. Will-Power

AN act of will is an act of choice, but few realize that our choices are made almost completely in line with our fundamental character. Except in the rare case of conversion or some other dynamic mental stress, we make our choices only in line with the sum-total of our mental habits, customs, ideas, and ideals. We are rarely able to muster will enough to act contrary to that which is usual with us. If we have always taken coffee for breakfast and have looked upon it as the natural thing to do, we find it almost impossible to give it up completely and instantly simply because we suddenly find it would be better to do so. The same is true of sweets, fattening foods, alcohol, tobacco, late-sleeping, or any other habit. We may have a very strong "will" to change, but we find that this sudden determination or concept is no match for the acquired habit. Our tendency to think and act in a contrary direction is stronger than the new idea. As Coué has shown, the imagination has cultivated the expectancy of these things, and is stronger than the will. "Whenever the will and the imagination come into conflict," he says in substance, "the imagination always wins." We cannot force the subconscious by an act of will for it is moved upon by mental pictures. We can control it only by controlling the imagination. He illustrates by saying that a man can easily walk a narrow plank when it is on the ground because his will to do so and his imagination that he can are in harmony. But let the plank be elevated in the air between two buildings and ask the man to cross, and though it is his will to do so, his imagination pictures him as falling off, and in the vast majority of cases he either gives up the attempt, or gets down and crawls.

A short time ago one of our "human spiders" was advertised to give an exhibition of climbing one of our high buildings. On the morning of the performance he awoke with the feeling that he could not do it. He told his wife, much to her surprise, as he had given many such exhibitions and had never shown the least fear. She therefore encouraged him to go on as the people would be disappointed as well as those for whose benefit it was being done. He went with reluctance. As he was climbing by the window of one of the upper stories a lady heard him say to himself, "I can't do it. I can't do it," and she laughed because she thought it merely a bit of humor. But before he had reached the top, he was seen suddenly to falter, his hand slipped, there was a gasp, a cry from the crowd, and he fell to his death on the pavement below.

In this instance we see the result of the conflict between the will and the imagination. While he had previously acquired the habit of thinking of himself as able to make such a climb, in this case he had lost the subconscious impression, and the new but ruling idea that he could not climb dominated his movements and brought on his failure and death.

It can be seen from this just what the method of procedure must be for the cultivation of will control. It lies in nothing else than in the formation of habits along the line of the desired attainment. It means cultivation of the imagination of one's self in the ascendancy as we found in the foregoing chapter, and in the habit which follows upon a consistently cultivated imagination.

We all have in us the potential Dr. Jekyll and also the potential Mr. Hyde and each acts in consonance with his character. But finally the strongest concept rules and either we become all Dr. Jekyll or we become, as in the story, all Mr. Hyde. The subconscious mind is thus graphically represented, and we can see the necessity of the cultivation of those ideas, concepts and imaginations that lead to a character which tends in the direction toward those higher choices we shall be called upon to make.

It is largely therefore a matter of the acquisition of right habits. The primary factors in the change of habits and therefore of character are the following:

1. Sincere desire for a change.

2. The devotion of the necessary time to meditation and practice.

3. The selection or choice of what we want to do or become, or the habit to be acquired.

4. The making of a resolution and who will accomplish it.

5. The practice of imagination, picturing, or visualizing ourselves as acting now along the line desired.

6. Definite rejection of contrary pictures or dwelling upon the negative side.

7. Cultivation of the "habit" of self-control and willpower in small ways, such as the voluntary surrender of little things over which the imagination of ourselves as in control can be easily conceived.

8. Insistence with one's self not to yield even once to the mental habit from which we wish to be free, or to the old ideas which are opposed to the new.

9. Meditation upon the higher self and the cultivation of the spiritualized consciousness as noted in the foregoing chapter.[22]

---

[22] Much help can be gained from a study of the chapter on Habit in "Psychology" by William James.

Chapter 19 SECRETS OF SUCCESS:
12. Obedience and Loyalty

WE shall not dwell on this requisite to success, as the principle is embodied in what we have already said. But we feel that a word should be said both for caution and encouragement. The newer order of thinking has done much to emancipate the mind and body from the old thralldom to antiquated customs, conventions, superstitions, creeds, and opinions. It has shown the primitive freedom of the spirit and the original and native sovereignty of the individual. It has demonstrated the necessity of initiative and originality as opposed to uniformity and conformity. But at the same time, it must not lead to iconoclasm. We must not be mental bolsheviki, repudiating the principles necessary to the solidarity of society.

The customs of society have their place and value. The laws of society are in general the solidification of the habits of the people into a code of social conduct which will be of advantage in our mutual contacts. It has been found, for example, that the feudal system of revenge as between families and individuals, in which one life is taken for another ("an eye for an eye and a tooth for a tooth"), is to the disadvantage of society. An offense, against one member of society is a menace to the safety of all, and, therefore, organized society or the state should take revenge or punishment into its own hands and mete out justice to the offender. It is to the advantage of all as well as to each, that men should not cheat or lie to each other. If we cannot trust each other, we have no way to transact legitimate business, suspicion will reign, business will become disorganized, and chaos will be the result.

Therefore it is incumbent upon each to become obedient to the moral, ethical, and social laws which govern the intercourse of all. And no man has a right to break these laws in order to gain a personal advantage. In doing so he inflicts an injury on all, and ultimately it must come back to him because still others will follow his method and throw society into such chaos as to destroy mutual confidence. When confidence is destroyed we have a state of anarchy, finance and credits fail, and poverty and want follow hard on the red track.

Business success demands obedience to the rules of the game, to the principles of the business, to the integrity of the organization. Every business is like an individual. It is literally an incorporation, that is, in a body. The eye cannot say to the hand, "I have no need for you."

Obedience to the rules is loyalty to the concern. And it is a truism that unless there is obedience there cannot be leadership. No man is worthy of leadership who cannot be a good follower. Indeed, he will find no one who will follow him. If, therefore you would become a leader learn to be a faithful follower. This does not mean sycophancy, it does not mean the prostitution of one's greater gifts, but it does mean reliability. And it is upon reliability that the success of the firm must be established.

I therefore place obedience and loyalty high in the scale of requirements for him who would carve out a successful career for himself and become a power in the world of business and finance.

Chapter 20 SECRETS OF SUCCESS:
13. Persistence

MOST of us recall the allegory of the turtle and the hare, how one was pitted against the other in a race, to the great amusement of the hare. With one bound the hare is away down the track, sailing joyfully over the rough places which the turtle must cover painfully, inch by inch. As he skims along he thinks to himself, "How easy this is! Poor dull turtle, he will never get anywhere." After a while he slackens his pace. There's no hurry. Let the turtle scramble along as fast as he can. He is so outdistanced, he cannot be seen. And so the hare decides to take a comfortable nap. He sleeps. He wakes yawning. It is later than he had thought. He looks back for the turtle. Nowhere in sight! He glances lazily ahead. What is that dark spot just at the finishing line. He leaps forward in a panic and comes up just in time to see the turtle reach the winning goal.

This story is an apt one. It reveals a secret of success. The race is not always to the swift. It is not always to the strong. The chaplet often adorns the brow of some obscure contender who persists to the end. As James says, "He that persists to the end, the same shall be saved," he who "holds on," who "fights it out on this line, if it takes all summer."[23]

Persistency begets reliability. The employer says, "Smith is a live-wire, and I would leave him in charge, but we do not know his sticking powers. Jones is slow, but you know how it is: he always sees things through to the finish. Better leave Jones on the job."

Persistency builds up traditions about the personality. The very earnestness and fidelity of the man who has it inspires admiration and confidence. It is one of the assets of maturity because both associates and acquaintances have come to rely upon it. It is a part of character and therefore has a real commercial as well as personal value.

The quality of persistency has not been always sufficiently noted in the Jewish race, which is the financial race par excellence. The "stick-to-it-iveness" of the Hebrew is an object lesson to those who seek advancement in vocation or business.

---

[23] Grant's words at the siege of Vicksburg.

Every periodical of modern times carries the story of some American who has attained success and who owes his present elevation largely to this quality.

From the standpoint of mental science the idea of persistency is the idea of constant and repeated suggestion. The mental attitude is, "I can succeed. I am going to succeed. I shall eventually get what I am after. I may be delayed, but I shall arrive. It is true that I haven't arrived but I'm on my way."

We are told of a newsboy who was offering papers for sale and thrust one under the eyes of a capitalist who was alighting from his car. "Paper, sir?"

"Get out of my way, brat, get out. No!"

"Say, Mister," said the lad, "you don't need to act so big. The only difference between you 'n' me is, you are on yer second million 'n' I'm only on me first."

Come on! You are on your first million at any rate. Success lies before you. Indeed, you are a success now if you are pressing forward cheerfully faithfully, and consistently toward the goal.

Chapter 21 SECRETS OF SUCCESS:
14. Cheerfulness and Courage

THE habit of good cheer is one of the greatest assets of success. No matter what of plenty may come to us, if we have not been each day extracting the full flavor of what we now have we cannot be said to have succeeded in the real business of living. How many there are of whom it may be said, "They spend so much time making a living that they have no time to live." They have kept their mind only on the work, only on the problem, only on the friction, only on the worry.

One can decide on which side of the road he will travel. There is a gloomy side and there is a sunny side. Two people working at the same job can often be seen traveling the same road—but on opposite sides. The cheerless one lives in the world of friction, care, burdened responsibility. There is always a cloud if one searches the sky, and it is not difficult to scrape up two! In one of her lectures, Harriet Louella McCullom tells of coming in one day to find her mother very much depressed. "What's the matter, mother?" she called out gayly. "Keep still, daughter," was the peevish answer, "But what's the trouble, mother?" "There you go again, oh, dear! you've made me forget what I was worrying about!"

The influence of cheerfulness upon success is well shown in time of war. Dr. Alexander Irvine told me one day how he was called by Lloyd George in an important crisis of the war to go to France and make speeches to "the boys" to keep up the morale. For several years he was whisked up and down the lines in an automobile, pumping out of his great heart the life-giving stream of good-cheer, of faith, and optimism which did so much to inspire the six million men who heard his voice.

What is morale but cheerful expectancy, the belief in one's cause, and the conviction of its triumph?

The optimist says, "It might be worse." The pessimist says, "It's going to be." The former encourages, "We'll pull out." The latter answers, "We can't. I'm all in."

When I was in Providence, Rhode Island, I learned of an old lady whom they all call "Auntie," who has the cheerful habit of saying, "It might be worse." One day a young man said to her, "Auntie, I had a fearful dream last night." "That's too bad, sonny, but it might have been worse." "But, Auntie, I dreamed I died." "It might have been worse." "Oh, but I dreamed I went to hell." "Too bad, sonny, too bad; but it might have been worse." "Why, Auntie, how could it have been worse?" "It might not have been a dream!"

I do not suppose that every cloud has a silver lining, but the vast majority of the clouds we see are not so black nor so dangerous as we allow ourselves to imagine. It may be only heat lightning we see and there is no danger of a bolt striking us, yet many rush to the cellar and hide in the coal bin. How much better to say with Lincoln in even the darkest hour, "This too shall pass away."

Let the howlers and professional pessimists go on with their howling. Let them yowl! Even at the midnight hour, lie still, and someone else will hurl his boots and brushes into the back yard, and you will be spared in three ways. 1. The noise will cease. 2. You will be saved from getting up. 3. Your boots will be ready for you in the morning.

Cheerfulness will enable you to see the brighter side, even though not the funny side. I do not recommend the trifling attitude of mind that makes a joke of everything. We need not be shallow and we need not be cynical, but we can be cheerful and courageous.

Above all we can exercise care in the choice of our companionships and our newspapers. There are minds whose thoughts run in turgid streams, there are papers across whose pages the yellow filth of the social gutter is allowed to spread; but the efficient prophylactic is a refusal to hear or see that which exudes its unwholesome contagion.

Cleanness, cheerfulness, courage! Against this wall of defense the "slings and arrows of outrageous fortune" will be blunted and broken.

Do not accept the negative into your consciousness for you begin to express what you think. If others say that times are hard, that the way is dangerous, that the future is black, let them accept their own suggestions, buy their own stove polish, and spill it all over the house.

"Somebody said that it couldn't be done,
But he, with a chuckle, replied
That maybe it couldn't, but he would be one
Who wouldn't say so, 'til he tried.
So he buckled right in with a bit of a grin
On his face. If he worried, he hid it;
He started to sing as he tackled the thing
That couldn't be done, and HE DID IT!

"There are thousands to tell you it cannot be done,
There are thousands to prophecy failure,
There are thousands to point to you one by one
The dangers that wait to assail you.
But just buckle in with a bit of a grin.
Just take off your coat and go for it.
Just start in to sing as you tackle the thing
That cannot be done, and YOU'LL DO IT!"

Chapter 22 SECRETS OF SUCCESS:
15. Good-will and Friendship

BUSINESS is built on confidence—the faith men have in one another. This faith is usually the result of the long-established integrity of the firm or one or more men associated with it. In the formation of new companies, the rule is to place in office and prominence those men whose "reputation" has been won for ability and honesty. "Bright young men" may carry the burden, but the name belongs to maturity and experience. One of the greatest assets of age is the standardization of capacity and also of friendship. In government and politics as a rule we find only the older men because they alone have built up the necessary associations, friendship, and established credits of personality.

In recent times we have seen a great deal of recapitalization of old firms going on, firms who have been manufacturing high-class products through the past fifty years or more. These firms have not only built up physical assets, in land, plants, goods, and so on, but they have great intangible assets, or what is termed good-will. The public believes in them. The name carries reliability. These assets cannot be spread on the books of the company, but they are paid for nevertheless. Scheming capitalists often buy an old company for the purpose of exploiting the name or goodwill of the firm. They reorganize, recapitalize, and sell up to fifty million dollars or more above the purchase price. The public invests on the "reputation" and integrity of the old firm, not knowing that the new one hasn't any. The profits of the concern must now be spread over the fifty millions of "watered stock" as well as the original twenty-five, so that the returns or dividends are only a fraction of what they were.

This illustrates the selling value of good-will, and while it carries with it a sacred responsibility so that no recapitalization should be allowed to take place except in the interests of an expanding concern, still we must see that the "good-will" is a commercial asset.

The art of creating good-will toward the firm by which one is employed and friendship toward oneself is one of the finest qualities of business and personal life. It carries its reward with it, for "a man's life consists not in the abundance of the things he possesses."[24]

ACQUIRING GOOD-WILL
In the acquirement of it some principles should be borne in mind:

---

[24] Luke 12:15 .

1. Honesty is an essential to good-will. When John Wanamaker began his career, he found that the custom of retail merchants was to set a price on an article well above the amount they really expected to obtain. Then a series of bargaining was carried on with the customer and after the necessary amount of haggling, the garment was sold. But this often left the buyer very much dissatisfied. Wanamaker determined to tag everything with the exact price and to sell at that price and no other. Other merchants thought it the part of folly. But as soon as the public became used to it, they appreciated uniformity and, having bought, they felt satisfied. The success of the plan needs no comment.

2. Courtesy. Few people can resist the charm of courteous consideration. The buyer has a right to expect it but he does not always get it. The rich demand it, and the poor appreciate it, if it is not mere condescension. It warms up human life and many a great man owes his greatness to the appreciation of those who have been charmed by his "human kindness." It puts people at their ease and many appreciate it without knowing just why they feel the pleasant glow that warms them.

Nothing alienates more than the feeling that one is being "put in the wrong," suspected of false motives, and so on. Marshall Field established it as a principle of good business that "the customer is always right." Even though occasional loss might be suffered, still, in the long run, the increase of good-will more than repaid the deficit.

In the ordinary affairs of vocation, profession, or social life, it will be found a good principle to acquire the art of putting people at their ease, physically and mentally. Nothing shows a greater charm of personality than the ability to meet men and women of every walk of life and be one with them. In the language of Paul, "I am all things to all men." This does not mean either to talk up or to talk down; it means to take the mental position that we are all equal on the plane of humanity; we are all men and women, and we take each other on the level of man to man.

3. The cultivation of memory of faces and names. This observation is hoary with age but is eternally true— people feel complimented if you remember them, doubly so if you recall their names. To give them title is to raise them at once above the dead level of the unknown and inconspicuous. One's name has a great charm to him. It is his distinguishing mark, his title, his claim to individuality. With what romance he himself endows it; what depth of meaning there is to it. He is not Smith, he is Smythe. He is not O'Toole, he is O'Doole. The O'Tooles are a common lot, they are low in the social scale, but his name is famous in the annals

of the clans. "There was a Sir James O'Doole in the army of King Richard," and — —

And you must pronounce the name right even if its owner pronounces it wrong. Respect a man's name and he will respect you.

4. The necessity of friendship. Friendship does not thrive on an empty stomach. It has appetite. It needs feeding. One must be always a friend. Fair-weather friendship is no friendship. Convenience never enters into it. It is not a profession, it is a principle. It is not an accountant and it never carries a balance sheet. It accepts gain or loss with equal grace. It demands nothing. It endures everything. It is blind in the right eye.

The spirit of friendship is genuine liking for "folks." Not merely our folks but your folks. It has nothing to do with the dinner grace of the man who prayed,

> *"Lord, bless me and my wife,*
> *My son John and his wife,*
> *Us four and no more."*

If you like people, they will know it. You will not need to advertise it, nor write a letter about it. If there is enough love in the heart, it will appear of its own self on the face. It cannot be painted on or "made up."

If you lack friends, it is because you lack the spirit of friendship, which is nothing less than a hearty interest in others, an instinctive desire for their welfare, and a sincere pleasure in becoming one of those who contribute to it.

In my psychology lecture tours I am constantly approached by those who claim that they have no friends, that those whom they have won have shortly been lost and that they cannot make new ones. Such a situation is incredible. It is not due to the neglect of the world, but to the lack of some quality in those who make the complaint.

I have seen aged women, left alone in the world, without material possessions, without beauty, faced by hardship, whose lives are beautiful when viewed in the light of friendship. They draw it, they hold it, they radiate it. So we see that it is not a material quality that is necessary. It is not the ability to confer a benefit. It is an understanding spirit. It is an unselfish heart.

A study of the psychology of those who lose their friends and are unable to attract others, reveals the fact that there is a flaw in the fundamental character. Claims have been made on the ground of friendship — demands, censure, gossip, judgment, criticism, claws. Friendship does not thrive on these. It is not the province of friendship to pick out the vices but the virtues.

"But," someone objects, "is it not the part of honest friendship to point out our friends' mistakes?" "Well," I answer, "what results have you obtained by your method? Did your friend change his habits or his friend? Who profited by your frankness, you or he, or neither?"

"Then should we let our friends get themselves into trouble when a word from us might save them?"

"The question is, 'Does it?' "

It is true that there are some who can correct their friends and "get away with it," but if you have found you do not belong in that rarified atmosphere of friendship, leave advice to those who are qualified to give it.

The real trouble, however, lies in the subconscious mental attitude, which is that of unacknowledged jealousy of one's friends or a heathen "I told you so" feeling when they go wrong or get into trouble, or an unexpressed but real spirit of censure.

Can your love and friendship bear up under the scrutiny of those subtle qualities which St. Paul declares are the demand of real love? "Love suffereth long and is kind: love envieth not; love vaunteth not itself, is not puffed up, doth not behave itself unseemly, seeketh not its own, is not provoked, taketh not account of evil; rejoiceth not in unrighteousness, but rejoiceth in the truth; beareth all things, believeth all things, hopeth all things, endureth all things. Love never faileth."[25]

The solution of the problem of friendship can be found by a careful and honest analysis of oneself in the light of what has just been said. Take each suggestion and meditate upon it. "Do I mentally pass judgment upon my friends?" "Do I suffer long and remain kind," or am I rather in the habit of giving people a "piece of my mind?" And if I do can I spare it? "Do I take no account of evil?" Is my interest in friendship without a "string to it"?

Then carefully eradicate from the mind all the negative characteristics. Pull out all the old weeds. Clean the mind up. Make yourself fit for friendship. Then use counter autosuggestions. "I am filled with the spirit of friendship and good-will. I love 'folks.' I am friendly. I have friends. I am in the midst of friendship."

---

[25] I Corinthians, 13:4-8

Mentally picture yourself as surrounded by companions, as enjoying the fellowship of others, as having confidants. Make yourself a mental magnet which draws others to you.

Then go out to the world of people around you who are just as hungry for love and friendship as you are and, without strain, in perfect naturalness, without self-consciousness, and in the sense of freedom from the necessity of any effort or any need, give yourself heartily to social contacts. Soon you will find yourself under the sweet sway of another's charm. Accept it, admire it, imitate it, respond to it and to all advances, and presently you will find that others are drawn to you as you are drawn to them.

5. Avoidance of antagonisms. It is very easy and very fatal both to friendship and good-will to put others on the defensive either by arguing too much, asserting too much, or claiming to know too much. The man who has knowledge is often tempted to use it where it is unnecessary. He is inclined to force it upon another, colored with his own opinion. "The know-it-all" and the "smarty" is actually offensive, even though his knowledge is genuine. There is a natural combativeness in every man or woman and it is easily aroused by over-strong assertions. And it is not easy to allay it once it is aroused. In innumerable instances salesmen have been found actually arguing with their

customers, the latter even taking the defense of the goods of a competitor, not from any preference for the goods, but with the firm determination not to get the worst of the argument. I have often seen men and women in just this situation in social and business life and even noted the woman dissolving into tears immediately after because she had been forced into the position of putting up a defense for something in which she did not herself believe. What a fatal mistake for both parties! How destructive to good-will and understanding! To win an argument is an empty victory when it leaves the goods unsold, the friend irritated, and the seeds of further friction already sown.

Let us not forget that we are all engaged in the business of living and that what we have said applies to it as definitely as to trade.

6. This spirit of helpfulness is essential to the creation of good-will. We cannot rate this too high for after all salesmanship itself is a form of service. The object is to present something that will be of real value to the purchaser, and contribute to his well-being and happiness. Salesmanship is merely the method of helping him to a decision. Anyone can take an order or pull the goods off the shelf, but it is a fine art to enter sympathetically into the life of another in such a way as to feel his needs, desire to satisfy them; and honestly to help to their gratification, without exercising

compulsion or interfering with the freedom of his personality. If the idea of service is held above everything else, the man who lives by it will win, in the long run, over all so-called competitors, because he will have established a reputation for reliability—and it is this reputation which we have denominated goodwill. Goodwill is an undistributed dividend. It is not cash but it is potential cash and it is wealth. Friendship is wealth.

Chapter 23 SECRETS OF SUCCESS:
16. Tact

ONE of the great secrets of success is tact. It takes skill to move to a definite point without arousing antagonism and, above all, to avoid the necessity of taking issue with another whose ignorance, prejudice, or bombast seek to browbeat you out of your position. Neither to capitulate nor to antagonize! O Tact, what wonders are accomplished in your name! What marvels of mental adroitness! Skill. Wit. Knowledge of facts. Tolerance. To know when to talk and when not to talk! To know when to listen as well as when to speak! To talk just enough and no more! To reverence silence as you reverence eloquence! To value words fitly spoken but not to be hypnotized by your own!

One must note the impression his speech is making and be guided by it. He should if possible draw out the opinion of his customer but only at such points as will reasonably assure him that they will be of an affirmative character. Another's opinion may be very valuable especially if he is well-informed, but the hour of a sale is not the school hour and the main object should never be forgotten.

Tact demands a knowledge of another's character, his probable point of view, his general interests. It is the part of wisdom to know all you can about a customer in advance, what his hobbies are, and especially his eccentricities. To mention a man's diversions might lead to opposite results; in one case to pull you in and in another to throw you out. The "hard-headed business man" may have imagination enough to know that you are simply using "salesman's tactics" when you run your eye over his wall and become suddenly enthused by his portly form in a pair of knickers. His stuffed fish may recall to him a different story from the one you have in mind. He may be more interested in what you have to sell than in what you think of golf, and the mere mention of a club may suggest its usefulness. It takes tact to determine these delicate points. Some men are very sensitive about their golf.

Nevertheless a friendly spirit usually awakens a response in another, leading to sympathetic relationships. This is as true in one walk of life as it is in another.

Never forget that it is a part of tact in any intercourse where you have an end to gain for yourself to show the other what he is to gain for himself.

One of the fine points of tact is the way you deal with yourself. It is very hard to admit a fault to yourself. A dozen alibis readily present themselves. Or discouragement sets in. "Of course I am a 'boob'; there's

125
CSLAsheville.org

no use trying." What adroitness it takes to correct yourself and still remain self-confident, "sold to yourself!" Nevertheless this is demanded. If you have failed in an undertaking where good salesmanship is a deciding factor, ask yourself afterwards why you failed, and what you should have done. Make up your mind it will not occur with you again.

Nor should we forget that we are all salesmen, selling our services, our goods, our personality, to society, the church, the club, the lodge. We are all interested in "putting ourselves over to the public," and success demands the acquisition of the art.

Chapter 24 SECRETS OF SUCCESS:
17. Bigness and Detail

THE quality of "bigness" must be associated with the successful mind. Great men in any business, vocation, or profession must be big men—men who see things in the large, who rise above the petty and inconsequential, and employ their forces positively rather than negatively. To a "little" man, everything assumes an equal importance. He is "on his dignity," he must not be "slighted," he "cannot forgive the oversight," he expends nervous energy over trifles, he is intolerant of opposition, he suspects motives and resents them, he picks out the flaws, he fears ridicule, he sees things "in the small" rather than "in the large," he ventures lamely, taps with his cane, and hugs the wall. The big man dares more, believes more, conceives more, puts others on their own responsibility, passes over but does not "pass up" detail, never does for himself what he can get another to do as well, forgets as well as forgives, does not argue, comes to definite decisions, acts forcefully, dares divinely, accepts delay or defeat calmly, is tolerant of other opinions even though constant in his own, is open to suggestion, willing to change to a better policy, sees much, hears more, and talks less.

Measure your mind against these requirements and see how "big" you are. Bigness does not exclude detail.

Attention to detail is not the mark of smallness. A big man can attend to little things in a big way. If detail is his work, he can make it a perfect service. He can make the office of a filing clerk the pivot of the whole business. He can be a library of information, an indispensable factor in the smooth running of the machinery. Many failures can be traced to lack of attention to detail, such as delay in answering correspondence, laxity in accounts, improper methods of filing data, carelessness in meeting obligations. To these the man who would succeed should turn his attention. "A little leak will sink a great ship." How much sooner will your frail bark go down if you disregard the essentials of your career?

Resolve to be faithful in little things in order to be made a "ruler over many things," but at the same time launch your soul out on the sea of life in the big way. Practice seeing things "in the large." Overcome pettiness. Control your "feelings." Cultivate generosity in your dealings with and estimate of others. Resolve on the big issue.

"God give us men! A time like this
demands,
True hearts, strong heads and ready hands,
Men whom the love of office cannot buy,
Men who have honor, men who will not
lie.
Strong men, who live above the clouds.
Of petty policy and private thinking,
Men who can damn a selfish demagogue
without blinking,
For while base tricksters with their worn-
out creeds,
Their base professions and their little
deeds,
Wrangle in petty strife, lo, freedom weeps,
Wrong rules the land and waiting justice
sleeps"

Chapter 25 SECRETS OF SUCCESS:
18. Knowledge of the Laws of Suggestion

ONE of the most startling discoveries of recent times is the fact that the greater part of the world lives and acts not on the basis of a self-chosen path but rather in accordance with the suggestions and impressions by which they are surrounded. We have seen that as between will and imagination, the latter always rules and we have found out the reason why. We should add to this the further fact that mental pictures and ideals are being constantly presented to us in the way of suggestion without our conscious thought. Anything may be denominated a suggestion which sinks into the subconscious or habit mind and produces a result either in the thoughts, feelings, or acts of the individual who receives it.

CONSCIOUS AND UNCONSCIOUS SUGGESTION
A conscious suggestion is one in which the individual consciously chooses some idea which he wishes to plant in the subconscious. The process of giving it is what we call autosuggestion or self-suggestion as in the famous phrase of Coué, "Day by day in every way I am getting better and better." All treatments and realizations given at the close of chapters in this book are therefore autosuggestions and are designed to

impress the subconscious mind with the idea of attainment leading to financial success.

But we are also receiving a constant bombardment of unconscious suggestion from our associates, society, the papers, and environment in general. Most great business depressions can be shown to be largely due to unconscious suggestion in which an ever-widening circle of the public joins, until it becomes an accepted idea that "times are hard, money is tight, business is getting poor, overexpansion must be followed by reaction which has now set in or is setting in, or is likely to set in." It is like "taking a cold," you have no cold now but you are "catching cold," you "feel it coming on," you "always have a cold after such an 'exposure'," etc. After the panic has been produced by the suggestion, a long period of mental and financial depression follows, and then the more venturesome minds "take a chance" in declaring that there is going to be an improvement. They are of course frowned upon, laughed at, and a concerted effort is made to suppress their enthusiasm. But if the idea is maintained, others gradually join, new ventures are set on foot, old ones are resuscitated, and "the boom is on," and "good times" result—from the suggestion.

POSITIVE AND NEGATIVE SUGGESTIONS
Many people are constantly giving themselves suggestions unconsciously. They are saying, "I cannot

do it. There is nothing ahead for me. I never 'get the break.' Something happens at the last minute. There's no use in trying." These and many other suggestions which will occur to the reader are negative or destructive unconscious suggestions, unconscious because the man who makes them does not know that every time he gives them utterance he is damning himself. In a sense, of course, all suggestions are affirmative rather than negative; that is, they are the affirmation of the negative. And to affirm a negative state is eventually to create it.

In general, it is better to speak of constructive and destructive suggestions, the former having the tendency to encourage, inspire, and create favorable action, the latter to produce in harmony, sickness, failure, distrust, and unfavorable action. Disease and failure are direct products of creative thought as truly as are health and success. All words, thoughts, and suggestions should therefore be carefully noted to see that they do not convey ideas contrary to constructive purposes.

DIRECT AND INDIRECT SUGGESTION
Suggestions may be made either directly or indirectly. It is often the part of wisdom to camouflage a suggestion. Great care has to be taken that those to whom they are given do not recognize them as such. There are many people who resent the idea of being

influenced by suggestion, as though in some way their personal liberty were being assailed; although as a matter of course no suggestion can ever become effective until it is an autosuggestion, and the trained mind need never accept those that are made. Indeed, one should suggest to himself, from time to time, that he is mentally wide-awake and that he will not act upon any suggestions of which he is not consciously aware.

However, there is a cross-grain in some natures which must be borne in mind when dealing with them. Like everyone else they are susceptible of suggestion but they always take the opposite side, and this must be met in the proper way.

Let us suppose that a woman is attempting to persuade her husband to take a trip with her. She knows in advance that if he thinks she really wants it, he will take pride in saying he simply cannot leave his business. She will perhaps discuss the nature of such a trip, how some of her friends have recently taken it, how much enjoyment they had from it, and conclude by saying, "But of course you won't have time for it next week." His testy reply is likely to be, "Why do you say of course? Where do you get that idea? Who said I didn't have time?"

"Oh, Alice and I were talking it over and she said she had a wonderful trip, but of course you wouldn't leave your business for it."

"What does she know about it? You're both wrong. I'm going."

We are not here recommending fiction, for there are always facts to fit the case.

Or we will suppose a family to whom the wearing of dinner clothes is only an occasional affair and the man of the house detests doing it. The wife does not say, "Now, dearie, be sure to put on your tuxedo." She knows too well what he will answer. She lays the suit on the bed and says, "Mrs. Jones phoned me it will be a formal affair."

A salesman often finds it profitable to use indirect suggestion as when he says, "Your neighbor Jones bought one of these washing machines because he says he isn't going to allow his wife to break her back over a washboard."

To "wonder how such a beautiful garment can be made for such a price?" is an indirect suggestion.

The above is very obvious but it illustrates a principle which the alert mind should know. Then exercise your own mental powers in creating suggestions to ease the pathway of your own life. It is important to remember that no one else can be your brains for you and no system is "fool proof." Practice and inventiveness alone will produce results. Get in the habit of watching yourself, or thinking about the suggestions you are making and how you can improve them.

FURTHER TYPES OF SUGGESTION

There are of course many types of suggestion. A combination of indirect suggestion and "sensory suggestion" may be found in the advertising value of doughnut-cooking in a window where the fragrance assails the nostrils, the sight delights the eye, and the whole appeals to the stomach. Sensory suggestions are also being constantly made within us as when we suddenly become conscious of some part of the body and dwell upon it with fear, wondering if it is the beginning of some disease, until we have built up, perhaps, the very condition we have feared. One should always refuse to worry over such matters. Either go to a practitioner, physician, treat it mentally until well, or forget it until it speaks in louder tones.

The opposite to sensory suggestion is psychic. Many have minds easily contacted by impressions and are able to "pick up" thoughts out of the atmosphere just as the receiving set of the wireless picks up the sentient pulsations of the ethers. One must be careful not to become an indiscriminate receiving set. Learn to tune out much that seeks admission to your mind.

Psychic impressions and suggestions are often made by the direction of the thought to any other mind near or far. These suggestions may be good, as in the case of mental treatment at a distance, or they may be distinctly destructive. A friend of mine one day gave a mental treatment for a man who was out of work, "broadcasting" the call for an employer, and within a few days he had seven offers of employment, some of them from other States. On one occasion the author remarked that one might mentally contact his friends whose whereabouts he did not know, and bring an answer to him. A young man in the audience came back in a couple of days and said he had followed directions and had heard from a friend whom he had lost track of for many months. On another occasion, the author told the story of this young man and a woman in the audience put the principle into practice to learn the whereabouts and condition of a friend. Within a few days she received a letter from the woman and information from four other different sources including a physician who was treating her friend. It is useless to argue here on the problem of coincidence. It has already been settled in a scientific way by authenticated cases as in the books of Flammarion.

Further consideration will be given in the second part of this book.

Remember you are living in a world of suggestion and learn to study the factors that control or influence your thought, conduct, and destiny. Are you affected by good suggestions or bad, positive or negative, optimistic or pessimistic, personal or impersonal, psychic or sensory, direct or indirect, voluntary or involuntary?

Then let me live to larger issues,
Let me put the small and petty by,
Let my mind triumph in its own control
And joy in conquest of its very thought.
Let me perceive and measure every breath,
Suggestion born, that blows upon me;
React alone to good, nor ill receive, or know.
I am the master of the inner world and so
The master of the world around.
My goal is Sure, my path lies to the heights

Chapter 26 SECRETS OF SUCCESS:
19. Work, Thrift, and Investment

THERE are two major ways of acquiring wealth from the commercial point of view,—man making money, and money making money. There is an infinite variety of ways in which this may be accomplished. From the standpoint of work there is the man who makes his living by the sweat of the brow. He is like the Irishman who is "digging the ditch to earn the money to buy the grub to get the strength to dig the ditch." This may be said, however, of any type of worker who spends, either from necessity or choice, all he earns. Second, there is the physical-mental worker who combines labor and mental skill, such as a foreman or a bookkeeper. Third, is the purely mental worker like the teacher. Then the mental-spiritual which is typified by the priest or clergyman. Finally, the spiritual service which is rendered to the race by the inspirer of emotions and ideals. And in this must be included those who—by the development and use of certain creative faculties, possessed by all but utilized by few—are able to bring wealth out of the Universal storehouse both for themselves and others. This quality, though little known, is not mystical and is fully explained in volume two of this series.

One of the great secrets of success is willingness to work, as we have already shown, and no system of moneymaking can be or ever was devised for the honest acquisition of wealth without work on some plane. Genius itself cannot create without lighting the candle; and art has a canvas back, a marble foundation, a brush and a chisel associated with it. We live in a universe of energy and some sort of energy accompanies every physical or mental act. "Genius," said Matthew Arnold, "is mainly an affair of energy."

Every theory has its field of practice and we commend this to those who are seeking to get something for nothing. They will get what they give, and if they give nothing they will get nothing. "Mental Science," says Judge Troward, "pays no premium on laziness."

But in the world of finance no great amount of income can be expected merely upon the day-by-day toil. There will be days when we do not toil, days in later life when we should not toil, and these must be provided for by the system which civilization has evolved of putting the surplus reward of toil to work in the form of capital. By the use of money, combinations of effort can be made through the bringing together of machinery, equipment, materials, and men. Capitalism is a necessary factor in industry, and he who provides any part of it should and does receive his share in its rewards.

But this means saving or thrift. There will be no surplus of the returns upon toil over the expense of daily living unless it is saved. If a man earns eight dollars a day and it cost him six of it for actual living, it can be seen that the two which he can daily save will in three days be sufficient to give him his living for the fourth. But he can put the two dollars to work and it will begin to create additional capital which in turn will go to work for him. Every dollar will soon give birth to a dime, and every dime is a baby dollar. America has learned the lesson of putting money to work but it has not sufficiently learned the lesson of thrift. We are, as a people, careless spenders because we have on the average so large a surplus above the necessities of life. However, it is not our thought to recommend mere self-denial but rather a system of living which will give us an equally high standard of living and still allow the accumulation of money to be used as capital.

Every child in the schools should be taught domestic accounting and the family budget system. He should not be preached at but taught how. We have already introduced thrift in the schools and through the post office; and we should stress the methods of thrift through careful accounting. This does not mean specialization as in the business college but merely simple bookkeeping showing the major expenses of home-making, and how they should be budgeted with relation to the income.

However those who are ambitious to increase their wealth can begin now to establish a budget and keep daily accounts with a view to making a definite daily saving and the accumulation of capital.

PUTTING MONEY TO WORK

The mere accumulation of capital is not enough, however.

To make money it must be invested or put to work. Money can be put to work in two ways. 1. Loaning it and receiving a rental value for it. 2. Investing it and receiving profits in proportion to the income.

When money is loaned the return upon it is fixed; if secured as in bonds or mortgages, it is reasonably safe; the returns are proportionally small.

Money that is invested rather than loaned does not carry the same security, but on the other hand it has an earning capacity. That is, your money goes to work with other money to produce a profit in which you yourself share. If all goes well with the business, you get paid not only for the use of the money but also for the risk and the business responsibility.

Invested money may go into your own business, in which case the two of you (yourself and money) are in a situation to realize large returns if your business is well-selected and you know how to run it. As only about ninety-five percent of business enterprises succeed in the long run, however, it is evident that only a small percent of people are properly situated for business adventure or have the business ability that is necessary. For this reason one should study himself honestly and scientifically and know that he has the twenty qualities of success herein described before he lends his capital to himself. It is frequently the poorest investment a man can make to invest in his own business and gamble on himself.

In such cases, and in all cases where the capital involved must be large, it is the part of wisdom to add your capital to that of partners or corporations in which the judgment and experience of others as well as yourself may be utilized. The most popular form of investment today is of course in companies incorporated for this purpose and run on the plan of giving each owner of the stock an authority in the management in proportion to his holdings. He can participate in the election of officers and executives.

The greatest earning capacity of money and the method which has produced most of the great fortunes of America has been that of investment in new companies, particularly for the development of natural resources. Money put to work in such companies has what is termed "creative power." H. L. Barber in his "Law of Financial Success," says:

"The creative power of money in new companies is really what makes men rich. This power is represented by the assets and good-will that the company acquires as it progresses in its business.

A million dollars may be put into a company as capital at the beginning. In a few years, after distributing a part of the profits as dividends, the remaining profits left in the business as further working capital may have increased the assets to $5,000,000, and the nature of the business may be such as to make the good-will worth another $5,000,000.

In this case, in addition to having the earning power represented by the cash dividends paid during these years, the original capital has multiplied itself in value ten times through its creative power.

If at this time the earning power is such that $1,000,000 a year may be distributed as cash dividends, the dividend rate will be 100 percent a year.

The company can now increase its capital from $1,000,000 to $10,000,000 and distribute $9,000,000 of stock as a 900 percent stock dividend, so that all the stock will draw a yearly cash dividend of 10 percent. Instead of getting 100 percent a year on one share, the shareholders will now get 10 percent a year on ten shares, the amount of money received being the same in either case.

If the company has prospects of continued growth in its business, these shares can now easily be sold at twice their par value. If the par value of the shares is $100 the person who bought one original share for that sum has ten shares of which he can sell nine for $1,800, and retain his original share. A few years later he may get another batch of dividend shares that he can sell in the same way.

The foregoing illustration of the idea is modestly drawn. It will be better to illustrate it with an actual case.

The Singer Manufacturing Company was organized in 1864 with a capital of $500,000, a large capital for those days. Stock dividends increased the capitalization, so that at the close of 1922 it reached $120,000,000. An original investment of $100 has, therefore, grown to $24,000 in stock. For many years these shares have sold in the market for very much above par.

Lately the dividend rate has been 7 percent, which would be an income of $1,680 a year on the stock now represented by the original $100 investment.

Up to 1914 the dividend rate was variable. In 1913 the $100 original investment drew $1,920; in 1912, $1,560; in 1911, $1,440; in 1910, $2,280; in 1909, $3,600; in 1908, $1,800; in 1907, $1,320; in 1906, $960; in 1905, $1,560; in 1904, $3,720, and so on back through the years, until in the earlier years it drew only from $50 to $100 a year.

The company has not included a financial statement in its yearly reports to the Manual of Corporations since the one for 1915. At the close of that year its assets were $125,471,000, and its surplus was $41,121,000.

It appears safe to estimate that its assets have grown, and increased in value at present prices, so that they now are fully $240,000,000.

In that case the $100 originally invested, now grown to $24,000 in stock, has a value back of it equal to $48,000, of which $47,900 represents what the creative power of this $100 has produced in these years, and we have seen that its yearly earning power now is about $1,680.

Money, then, has an earning power when it is put at work so that all it earns will go to its owner.

It has its greatest earning power when it is put at work where it will have a creative power."[26]

Most of the great enterprises of America have been founded on this method of capitalization, including railroads, steamship lines, telephone and telegraph, the great industrial plants, coal and metal mining. But while such investments are legitimate, since in no other way could most of the natural resources of the country be developed, still owing to the speculative element it is generally safer for those who cannot stand loss in case it should come to take the smaller income derived from the rental of money or purchase of "seasoned" securities. Many new concerns are constantly being formed headed by men whose ability and integrity have made successes of other businesses. The major requirements upon which to base a decision include knowledge of the efficiency and honesty of the management; the source of supply for the material or, as in the development of natural resources, the certainty of the undeveloped values; the cost of production or manufacture; the demand of the public for the product; and the probable margin of profit.

---

[26] Quoted by permission of author. "The Law of Financial Success," by H. L. Barber, note, p. 31.

Finally the question must be settled as to the certainty of sufficient capital to carry the business on until it reaches a paying basis.

Those questions must be satisfactorily settled before the investor can go ahead with an easy mind. If he cannot have an easy mind, he should not go ahead, but remain content with seasoned investments. Nor must the reader take the foregoing as approval of any particular investment that may be presented to him. It must not be forgotten that the large percent of new enterprises fail, but at the same time the fact should be clear that these failures are usually due to something that ought to have been foreseen, and also that this type of investment is the basis of practically all the large fortunes of America. It is for this reason that we have dealt with it at length as one of the factors in the attainment of financial success.

Chapter 27 SECRETS OF SUCCESS":
20. Moral Standards and Religious Faith

WE cannot believe that an untrustworthy personality is a success, however high he may be rated in Dun's and Bradstreet's. If a man's life consists in the satisfaction he takes in living (and no one can be said to truly live otherwise), then his own happiness must be affected by the question of integrity. Even though the world does not know of his dishonesty, he knows; and a sense of failure must come to him as he realizes that he won by "hitting below the belt"—of inferiority because he did not stand on the level with others and play the game according to the rules. Many a man recognizes himself as a failure although he is not so considered by others.

And deeper yet is the failure of him who is not conscious of moral obliquity, upon whom the lash of his own scorn does not fall as he views himself in the light of honest achievement; who is a coward and does not know it, a thief and does not see it, a liar and does not feel it.

In the long run "honesty is the best policy" because if we do not have a code of morals which applies to all alike, the standards of conduct are destroyed, every man's hand is against his brother, and social chaos is the result. The hard-won gains of civilization are those of moral and ethical achievement. Without those no permanent gain of wealth would be possible since the certainty of loss through the dishonesty of others would discourage effort.

The greatest menace to civilization lies not in bobbed hair, women's rights, "the problem of the sexes," the unearned increment, top-heavy fortunes, or taxes; it lies in the fading authority of the moral code. The ideals of men are as their gods and they both rule and ruin. They have the power of life and of death over our laws for our laws are but bodies in which our ideals are housed or embalmed as the case may be. First comes an idea or an ideal, which if agreeable is adopted as a general practice; then it becomes a custom; the custom is made uniform and finally prescribed; the prescription is the law. Laws, then, are built up out of the generally accepted ideas and ideals of a people. Sometimes we find the ideas or ideals have changed in which case the law is mummified, as in the proscription of the teachings of evolution, or the ancient statutes regarding Sunday observance. No amount of reactionary fanaticism can actually enforce an antiquated law of this kind because the ideas of society have changed. The same is true of new laws, written into the statutes before the ideas and ideals, which the laws seek to embody, have been sufficiently and generally accepted.

The greatest servants of society are not the law makers nor the law enforcers, but the law creators. The creators of laws are the ideas and ideals popularized and established in the minds of the people. For this reason, he who would reform society must reform its ideals. The great moral ideals of society, the rules of conduct, are in general embodied in the Ten Commandments, which history has worked out as the controlling force in personal and social character. Therefore we advocate the reconsecration of reformers, preachers, teachers, welfare workers, social reconstruction, etc., etc., to promotion of the moral and ethical code of the Ten Commandments. We believe that it has been a mistake to take the moral code out of the schools merely because it happens to be best expressed in the Bible. It was not given to us by the Jews. They had already borrowed it. It does not belong to any religion.

But this question of religion ought to be faced fairly in this connection. Why is the teaching of religion excluded from our schools? The major reasons are these:

1. We desire to separate religion and State, and as the school is a State institution, we do not wish to have religion brought under the domination of the State through the schools. It was to escape a State religion, that our forefathers came to America and declared the principle of religious freedom.

2. We desire to avoid the teaching of religious creeds, dogma, in the schools. As soon as one begins to interpret religion he is teaching theology. But each great religion and every branch of each religion has a different mode of interpreting its major principles. This forms sects, denominations, cults, and isms, in which each "ology" is different and presumably better than any other. Accordingly the Catholic opposes Protestant teaching, the Protestant opposes modernism or fundamentalism, as the ease may be, and both oppose ethnic religions.

Must we, therefore, rear half the population of America without religious training, since less than half attend churches? And must we develop a pagan race on the free shores of American whose moral ideals are uninspired by religion and perhaps untaught altogether? Or is there a way out?

It is our contention that the Ten Commandments can be taught in the public schools without giving offense to any religion. The religious background is, "The Lord, thy God (thy God, whether you be Jew or Gentile, Christian, Mohammedan, Buddhist, etc.), is One." Each race, nation, religion, or sect can say that of his God; He is One and no other is before Him. He demands the allegiance of every heart and it is His will and purpose that we obey the moral law. To violate the moral law is to place one's self in opposition to the will of God, out of harmony with the divine order and therefore in a position of personal peril. Not the peril of an angry God but the peril of those who have separated themselves from the source of power, guidance, and help.

The motivating power of morals is religion and religious responsibility. We cannot say that morality and ethics are instinctive; the training of childhood is the cataloging of do's and don'ts. The child is non-moral and non-ethical, but he is not non-religious. He is natively, instinctively, intuitively, fundamentally, and organically religious. The movement of his mind is naturally toward faith in God.

The instinct of worship is found in the very lowest races.

This native quality of the soul must be capitalized. It is in accordance with the deepest principles of psychology that we work always in harmony with the fundamental laws and instincts of mind to produce a desired result. Therefore to effect and enforce moral and ethical standards we should work in harmony with the fundamental instinct of faith and worship, fidelity to the code of conduct because it is the law and will of God. "The fear of God (that is, reverence and respect for His august authority) is the beginning of wisdom."

The mistake often made by reformers and politicians is the effort to seize upon religion as a sort of bludgeon. We hear them orating — and this runs clear up to the highest public authorities in the land — on the necessity of religion as a police force. But this is not the object of religion. The object of religion is to satisfy the human heart, to put meaning into life, to give strength to those who are weak in any respect, and to constitute a real brotherhood of the race through the common Fatherhood of One God. To attain this satisfaction, it is necessary to live in harmony with the source of it. One cannot be in such harmony who violates the wishes and the will of Him whose help they seek. But it is not a mere bargain, for there is a satisfaction in this state of harmony aside from any benefits that flow from it.

The child should be assured that his natural faith in God is rational, that others believe in God as he does, that his teacher believes in God; and so do the leaders of the community and national life. God should be an accepted fact of human and social life.

All this can be accomplished without any sectarian teaching, without any personal comment, simply by the repetition of the approved moral code which gives proper place for the supernatural.[27]

Such discussion may seem discursive but the psychological significance must not be lost. For whether the educational ideal here presented is accepted in the schools or not, the individual who seeks success must adhere to the scientific principle; fidelity to the moral code is essential and that code is rooted in religion. The motivating power of morals and ethics is faith in God. It is not blind faith, it is law. The law is that there is only one source for all things, one soil in which seeds of every kind are to be planted; and each will bring forth fruit after its kind, and no other. "You cannot gather grapes of thorns nor figs of thistles."

The soil in which these seeds are planted is the individual subconscious mind, the social subconscious, and the Universal Subconscious, with which we shall deal in Book II of this series. We must be in harmony with the Universal Principle which underlies and is fundamental to every principle whether financial,

---

[27] The use of the Ten Commandments is illustrative only. Another set of principles could easily be devised which all religions and creeds could accept as fundamental to their particular faith.

moral, ethical, or social. The fundamental principle of the subconscious is that the more refined the seed, the more refined will be the fruit. The higher the ideals, the words, the thoughts, the concepts, the purpose, the motive, the finer will be the product. Let us live and let us teach our young that "as ye sow ye shall also reap."

SUGGESTION

I am in harmony with and have faith in the moral order. I shall not be misled by the seeming possibilities of "the short-cut to success" through broken law of any kind. I am strengthened in my resolve to work out my problem and roach my goal in complete fidelity to social responsibility. I have faith in the triumph of right. I have faith in myself, faith in others, faith in God. I know that the law of mind cannot fail and that I shall not fail. I shall succeed, for I think success. I am success.

Chapter 28 CONCLUSION

THE reader will have no difficulty in figuring out the percent of his personal efficiency on the basis of the foregoing chapters. He can see himself more intimately than he is seen by others, and he can be governed accordingly. To some, the process may be more or less a discouraging one. On the other hand, it is hoped that courage has risen through the discovery that no matter how far now one may be from the ideal, still the power lies within him for its attainment. Jesus said, "Be ye therefore perfect, even as your Father in Heaven is perfect." One is potentially one hundred percent perfect, and it is to bring this potential into expression that we must all think and work

"Practice makes perfect"; constant effort to improve will bring its own reward. There is time to work out your problems, and age has nothing whatever to do with it. We might instance the lives of unnumbered men and women who have done "the big thing" after they had reached the age of fifty, or even eighty. What counts is the will to bigness. It is what you really want that counts. If you want it strongly enough, you will think about it, you will dream about it, you will work for it, you will develop capacity in regard to it, you will become an authority in it, you will be indispensable because of your knowledge, your reliability, and your enthusiasm. You will succeed

The great secret is the impregnation of your whole consciousness with the passion of your purpose. Fill yourself daily and hourly with the suggestion of success. "I am made of the stuff that masters problems. I have within me all the capacity I require. There is no such word for me as fail. I know only success. I believe in success. In my mind I am already a success, and I know that whatever I am within I shall sooner or later express without. 'I do not need to struggle, I only need to know.' It is knowledge and not struggle that will bring results to me. I shall not worry. I shall not drive myself. I shall be calm, expectant, steadfast.

Today I launch my soul out into the bigness of things. I set my sail and I steer my course to the great goal of my desire I sail fearlessly and independently. I sail joyously and gloriously. I am master of my fate."

"Today I set my soul the task
To go the way I will,
Today let all who wish me well
And all who wish me ill
Be still:
For I shall go as my soul decrees,
I shall sail for the harbors I choose;
It is I set the sail,
It is I face the gale,
It is I who must cope with the ruse
And the will of the storm
If I am to sail
Afar, without trail
Alone on the breast of the sea,
Can you turn the rudder for me,
Can you set my sail?
Can you meet my gale?
IS it you who shall take the blow?
Ah, then, is it well
That you seek to tell
Or dictate the way I shall go?
You may point me the light of a star,
You may warn of the reef and the bar,
You may say, 'It is so and is so,'
You may mark out a way I can go—
But you cannot sail it for me."

What greater independence of individuality can we ask than this, that no one can sail the sea of life for us. We trim the sheet to the wind, we hold the rudder, and we are away to the highest adventure the mind can conceive, the working out of our personal destiny, the development of our own inner resources, the expression of that which we feel ourselves to be. Life is self-expression

The ultimate nature of that self and its interrelationship with other selves through the common medium of the One Great Mind of the Universe will be considered in Volume Two of this series.

THE END

Made in United States
Orlando, FL
09 November 2024

53632600R00095